THE MOST NOTORIOUS JAILBREAKERS

Abeer Kapoor is a journalist and the creator of India's first election-based board game called 'The Poll', which was profiled by CNN, Vice, *The Diplomat* and several other national and international publications. He is a graduate of Azim Premji University, Bengaluru. His articles have appeared in *Hardnews*, The Wire, Scroll.in, *Quartz* and other magazines and websites. In his free time, he enjoys strumming the guitar, playing with street dogs and building new board games.

THE MOST NOTORIOUS JAILBREAKERS

UNTOLD STORIES OF ESCAPED CONVICTS

ABEER KAPOOR

RUPA

Published by
Rupa Publications India Pvt. Ltd 2020
7/16, Ansari Road, Daryaganj
New Delhi 110002

Sales centres:
Allahabad Bengaluru Chennai
Hyderabad Jaipur Kathmandu
Kolkata Mumbai

Copyright © Abeer Kapoor 2020

All rights reserved.

No part of this publication may be reproduced, transmitted,
or stored in a retrieval system, in any form or by any means,
electronic, mechanical, photocopying, recording or otherwise,
without the prior permission of the publisher.

The views and opinions expressed in this book are the author's own and
the facts are as reported by him which have been verified to the extent
possible, and the publishers are not in any way liable for the same.

ISBN: 978-93-5333-799-5

First impression 2020

10 9 8 7 6 5 4 3 2 1

The moral right of the author has been asserted.

Printer at HT Media Ltd, Gr. Noida

This book is sold subject to the condition that it shall not,
by way of trade or otherwise, be lent, resold, hired out, or otherwise
circulated, without the publisher's prior consent, in any form of
binding or cover other than that in which it is published.

Contents

Introduction vii

1. Daniel Hailey Walcott Jr — 1
2. Natwarlal — 11
3. Charles Sobhraj: How to Run a Prison and Walk Out of It — 23
4. Sukur Narayan Bakhia: Hide-and-Seek — 35
5. Mir Laik Ali: Getting Our Man Out — 48
6. Nabha: Gangsters, Terrorists and the Systemic Rot — 60
7. The LTTE Escape: Escape or a Cover-Up? — 73
8. The Burail Jailbreak: An Endless Tunnel of Official Oversight — 83
9. Sher Singh Rana: Higher Calling? — 95
10. Geeta Parmar: Karate Escape! — 108
11. Bitihotra Mohanty: 'Call Me Raghav Ranjan' — 113
12. Operation Jailbreak — 126
13. The Nawada Jailbreak: A Tale of Two Gangsters — 138
14. Walking Out of Prison — 149
15. POW: They Just Wanted to Go Home — 160
16. Psycho Killer: Thank God He Is Dead — 171

Acknowledgements 182

Introduction

When the opportunity to write this book presented itself, I was excited, to say the least. As a reporter who covered crime, I had to disengage myself from the news cycle so that I could take my time, pause and sink my teeth into each case of prison break. I studied the convicts' motivations from a variety of sources, including books, newspapers and, of course, talking to and interviewing people. What I did not, however, anticipate was the time and energy it would require to detach myself from each of the characters mentioned in this book. I needed time and space to get over the protagonist of one chapter before moving on to the next. It was not just their actions but also how they built their reputations and personalities from the crimes they committed. Psycho Shankar, for instance, was particularly hard to recover from. I could not digest the ease with which a 'family man' could commit one heinous crime after another, such as rape and murder, and yet have no regrets. Besides, it was also fascinating to note how prisons are a world unto themselves. Shankar's escape was possible probably because he had understood the language of the prison, and this is true across many cases.

In this book, you will encounter some really 'bad' people—from caste-based gangsters to smugglers, Maoist commanders, a serial killer and Pakistani soldiers. You will also meet their friends and suspicious police officers and be a witness to criminal official oversight. Of the 16 escape stories, at least two do not involve habitual or hardcore criminals. These two escapees were incarcerated because they got unlucky. These were Jawaharlal Nehru University (JNU) students of 1983 and Mir Laik Ali, the then prime minister (PM) of Hyderabad State.

The cases mentioned here range from the late 1940s to contemporary times. Smugglers such as Sukur Narayan Bakhia, Daniel Hailey Walcott Jr and Charles Sobhraj in the 1960s and '70s are also mentioned here. From the 1980s and early '90s, there are cases related to militant subnational forces, including the Liberation Tigers of Tamil Eelam (LTTE) and the extremist organizations from the Khalistani movement. From the early 2000s, this book explores the cases of caste-ridden rivalries in Bihar and Uttar Pradesh (Nawada jailbreaker Ashok Mahto and the killer of Phoolan Devi, Sher Singh Rana).

Each story of escape is driven by the main character and, of course, all those who aided the accused. It really takes a village and a little more to escape from prison. Bitti Mohanty, for instance, could not have escaped had it not been for his father (a Director General of Police-ranked officer in Odisha) and the vast network of willing and unaware aides. While some involve large terror and criminal networks, such as the Babbar Khalsa International (BKI) and the LTTE, most are spearheaded by the ingenuity and desperation of individuals for freedom.

The challenges in writing this book were immense: apart from poor archives and public records, prison files were not easily accessible. The biggest help came from the newspaper archive at the Nehru Memorial Museum and Library, New Delhi, as well as those of universities and open sources such as India Kanoon that provided me with the necessary material to dig deeper into the crimes.

The 16 stories are carefully selected. Most of these cases are long forgotten. The popular cases, on the other hand, are still talked about and being investigated or are very much part of public imagination, such as the Nabha and Burail jailbreaks as well as those of Charles Sobhraj, Natwarlal, Bitti Mohanty and Sher Singh Rana. Since information on these cases was readily available in the form of judgements and media reports, I felt like I was surrounded by a conveyor belt with various facts moving around me, and all I had to do was piece together a puzzle. In addition to historical and popular compulsions, I was interested in political escapees and their character traits. Unfortunately, due to poor documentation, I was unable to find much on escapes by the United Liberation Front of Assam (ULFA) in the Northeast.

Many of these notorious characters may have been lost to history or not got their due, but any lay reader will find the lives of those like Sukur Narayan Bakhia and Daniel Hailey Walcott Jr dangerously exciting. Both of them prospered to challenge the law-enforcement agencies at a time when a xenophobic India was a smugglers' paradise. Had it not been for its inward economic policies, these gentlemen would have been ordinary traders. None of these would have happened without the crumbling infrastructure of jails in India and the connivance of jail authorities.

Towards the end, it was a scramble to finish the book (the editors will laughably agree); the primary challenge was to not let the grotesqueness dominate the pages, but keep it fun. I hope to have achieved this. The editors, too, played a crucial part in making the copy sharper and more lucid. With incrimination, let me also share with you a five-step formula that I deduced to escape even the biggest jail in the country, and hopefully neither you nor I will ever have to try!

1. Find friends and accomplices.
2. Find a method (to dig a tunnel and sneak in those friends, etc.).
3. Pay bribes.
4. Pick a Sunday of your choice. (Many escapes have taken place on a Sunday such as Sobhraj's escape as well as those of Sher Singh Rana and Bakhia. Even the Operation Jailbreak, the Nawada Jailbreak and the Nabha Jailbreak happened on Sundays.)
5. Go for it!

one

Daniel Hailey Walcott Jr

On the morning of 8 June 1964, two pilots walked over the tarmac towards their Riley 65. It was 4 a.m., and according to the flight manifest, they were headed to Jask in Iran. It was a short flight. On clearing the Pakistani airspace, the pilot, Captain McLister, under the advice of his co-pilot, Captain Peter John Philby, took a sharp U-turn and headed towards the Indian coastline. They flew low, dipping below the radar, skimming the water as they kept clear of radar surveillance. The plane made its way to India carrying precious cargo—675 Swiss watches, the sale of which would provide them with ample funds to buy gold and smuggle it out of India.[1]

As the twin-engine plane approached the Indian coastline, McLister dropped altitude and began flying low, southwards along Bombay (now Mumbai). Philby kept his eyes peeled for two of his men, Jeno Csory Novak and Charlie Gillbanks, who were meant to flag the plane down with red and green saris

---

[1] Staff Reporter, '"Philby" None Other Than Walcott: Accomplice Throws Light on Escapade', *The Times of India* (1861–current), 8 July 1964; ProQuest Historical Newspapers: *The Times of India*, pg. 1

about 80 km down from the city. But as he searched, he found that neither of them had shown up.

The events that followed could have been lifted from a racy spy novel; from Steven Spielberg's *Catch Me If You Can* or even the classic American TV show, *The Man from U.N.C.L.E.* That morning, Philby and McLister found themselves out on Murud Beach, without their accomplices, surrounded by a group of puzzled locals and with nearly a million dollars' worth of smuggled watches. In that moment, Philby improvized. He pretended that they were flying enthusiasts from Amritsar who had lost their way and asked the local police to guard their plane while they left for Bombay to ask for help. Early next morning, they, along with Novak, who they had caught up with in Bombay, and the watches, boarded a flight to Karachi—deftly duping the Indian immigration security as well as Pakistan's—and from there to Paris.

As the details of this strange episode appeared in the newspapers over the next few weeks, it was debated in the Parliament. The Opposition was going hammer and tongs and accused the government of complicity, laxity and incompetence. The government approached Scotland Yard for assistance in the case, which now has come to be referred to as the 'Murud Plane Incident'. In the custody of the British police was McLister, who revealed that Peter John Philby was just an alias for Daniel Hailey Walcott Jr, who was not only on India's most wanted list then, but also the notorious international gold smuggler who ran a ring that spanned across Bahrain, Dubai, Hong Kong, Bangkok, Switzerland and India.

In fact, authorities in Lebanon had sentenced him to death for clicking photographs of their military installations and selling them to Israel.

THE NAME IS WALCOTT, DANIEL HAILEY WALCOTT JR

Born on 26 November 1927, in Dalhart, Texas, Walcott Jr's father was a geologist and businessman who kept the entire family on the move. Those peripatetic years exposed him enough to build a life he had not lived. So Walcott painted his childhood the way he liked. Once he claimed that he was the son of a judge, but actually, that was his grandfather. Another lie he would tell was that he was the descendant of Oliver Wolcott, a man who signed the United States's Declaration of Independence.

During the Second World War (1939–1945), he served in the American Navy, and after his service, he took admission in the University of Virginia. Although his razor-sharp intellect could have taken him anywhere, he dropped out as he wanted something else in life.

'Dan Walcott landed in the old-guard affluence of San Francisco as a young man in the 1950s,' wrote Joe Mozingo in the *Los Angeles Times*.[2] He described Walcott as a 'somewhat mystery man, a Gatsby-esque figure, not really belonging to the world he had come to inhabit'. Walcott was described as tall and slender, with piercing blue eyes. He was charming and debonair, with a stately charm.

According to Mozingo, Walcott married into a family that was part of the highest echelons of San Francisco's society. His father-in-law was a member of the Bohemian Club, a select club whose members included the likes of bankers, businessmen

---

[2] Joe Mozingo, 'Will the Real Daniel Walcott Please Stand Up?' *Los Angeles Times*, 11 March 2001, https://www.latimes.com/archives/la-xpm-2001-mar-11-tm-36078-story.html, last accessed on 6 November 2019

and even former United States (US) presidents. Patsy Browne, his first wife, didn't even know what Walcott did for a living. She thought he was a pilot, but that was not true of course.

Five years after his marriage, he set up a freighting company called the Trans Atlantic Airlines. He flew refugees in and out of countries, imported exotic animals into the US and slowly made his way to other parts of the world.

CAUGHT!

By 1962, Walcott's Trans Atlantic Airlines won a contract with Air India, and his planes started flying cargo from railway hubs all over India to Afghanistan and back. The Walcotts decided to make India their home for a while, and travelled through the country in his Piper Apache.

It is alleged that during this time Walcott sold bullets and cartridges to the rajas and princes of India's über-rich princely states, and was once caught smuggling rare items in the presence of an Indian chief minister.

On the night of 20 September 1962, from the moment the police barged into their room in Delhi's The Ashok Hotel, the American businessman knew that he was in a world of trouble. After searching their room and also the one in which his secretary was staying, the Delhi police recovered 766 ordinary gun cartridges and two emergency cartridges. On searching their plane, which was parked at Safdarjung Airport, they found 40 boxes of 250 cartridges each.

Walcott was arrested on charges of smuggling and violating the Arms Act, 1959. He was presented in the court of N.L. Kakkar, a subdivisional magistrate in New Delhi, and was immediately charged with smuggling, with intent to sell. The police also found four empty wooden boxes that they believed had more cartridges, a charge that Walcott denied. He was remanded under judicial custody and sent to Tihar. His planes were impounded and over the next year, he would spend time in and out of jail and courts all over India.

On 23 October 1962, shortly after being released on bail, he headed for Amritsar, from where he tried to escape from India, through the Wagah border, but was caught and brought right back to New Delhi, where he was put on trial again.

This time, Walcott adopted another strategy. India was heading towards a war with China, and in this moment, the American offered his planes to the war effort. His Douglas C–54 Skymaster was a decommissioned war plane. The magistrate took the offer into consideration, but sent Walcott back to jail anyway. His legal travails continued for a while, until he was finally let go: his jail term was reduced to time served and he was asked to pay bail.

There were, however, two problems: his planes were still impounded and he owed the Tatas over ₹60,000, as they had paid for his bail. In debt and without a plane, Walcott found himself in a tight spot.

Walcott was allowed to maintain and service his plane. He would go to Safdarjung Aiport every morning to fire up his Piper Apache. On the morning of 23 September 1963, much as he had done in the past week, under the watchful eye of the constable at the airport, Walcott sprinkled some fuel in the engine, went in and turned the key to bring it to life.

He had been in and out of prison in India for the past year, making short jaunts to neighbouring countries and always coming back. But now, the authorities were working on obtaining a non-bailable warrant for the Texan because he owed money to the Tatas and had not shown any intention to pay them back.

Aware of this, he went through the security, took out his plane to the tarmac, got in, revved it and before the constable on duty could find his bearings, started the plane towards the runway. There was an investigation on whether the officers on duty had been bribed by the American, but it remained inconclusive. Another strange anecdote is that a constable chased Walcott's plane and when he got close, Walcott turned on the wipers to squirt water on his pursuer.

The plane took off, and before leaving Delhi's airspace, it flew in a little circle over Tihar, allegedly dropping chocolates, cigarettes and other items for the inmates. Walcott made his way to Karachi, where, on landing, he immediately called for a press conference to complain about the ills of the Indian bureaucracy.

A SMUGGLER'S HAVEN!

During his short stint in Tihar, Walcott met a French gold smuggler, Jean Claude Donze. Together, they came up with a plan to smuggle in gold to India and through it built an international smuggling network that spanned across 20 cities[3] in two continents.

Walcott was useful to Donze for his flying skills while Walcott just wanted to live for adventure.

In post-Independence India, smuggling was commonplace. Nath Pai, a Member of Parliament (MP), said in the well of the Lok Sabha that India was once a place where thinkers and

---

[3] Anjali Chanda, 'India: Paradise for Smugglers', *The Times of India* (1861–current), 23 May 1971, pg. 2

intellectuals came to find a home for their ideas, but had become a place for smugglers.

India's western coastline was long, indented and porous. It had enough creeks, inlets and drop-off points that were used to smuggle in gold, watches, cigarettes and liquor into the country. According to an article in *The Times of India*, in 1971, over ₹400 crore of gold was illegally shipped into India.[4]

The bulk of smuggling was done by boats called dhows, which are sail boats that have ferried the route in the Indian Ocean for over 500 years. The report claimed that in 1971[5] these boats were used to bring all sorts of goods into India. The Arab ships (dhows) would moor off the coast and wait for Indian merchant crafts, who would then exchange the goods off the west coast and these ships would drop off the bounty in either Bombay itself or elsewhere along the coast.

This was what Walcott and Donze wanted to exploit. They would put advertisements up in newspapers on behalf of their several shell companies, lie to their pilots or hire them for their schemes. So on that June morning when they took off from Jask, they were making their way to India to exchange the 675 watches for gold. Gillbanks and Novak had found a buyer and it was a quick in-and-out operation, something they had done a couple of times by then.

CATCH ME IF YOU CAN!

Circling around the area, they had been flying for about an hour more than anticipated and were running on fumes. McLister

---

[4] Anjali Chanda, 'India: Paradise for Smugglers', *The Times of India* (1861–current), 23 May 1971, pg. 2
[5] Ibid.

had no other choice but to make a force-landing. He found a wide-enough beach and decided to force-land. Once it hit the soft ground, the plane went up on its nose and the propellers bent under the weight of the plane.

Philby jumped out fearing that the jerry cans filled with petrol would catch fire, and pulled a dazed McLister out. They landed in Murud Beach, some 230 km from Bombay. In India, for a small crowd to gather is not hard, and by the time they had managed to assess the situation, one had formed near them. Running away was no longer an option. The crowd forced them to trek to the nearest police station in Dapoli.

The two trekked to the station and brought back two police officers to the plane. They claimed to be flying enthusiasts who had taken off from Amritsar to land in Bombay, but had got lost along the way. A crowd of 20 had assembled by this time, one of whom was the district magistrate. They repeated the story to him and were ordered to have their bags checked.

Philby at this point convinced the district magistrate and the cops to stand guard over the plane while they got help from Bombay. The two took two suitcases filled with the contraband, got on a local bus and made their way to the city.

Six hours later, on reaching Bombay, they contacted Novak, and the three realized that they couldn't stay in India much longer without jeopardizing their operations and futures. There was, however, a problem. While Novak had a stamp on his passport on entering India, McLister and Philby did not. They stayed there till the next morning after which they made their way to Santa Cruz Airport. They found that a flight from Dar es Salaam had arrived, and as the passengers began to disembark and walk to immigration, Philby and McLister joined the group. The problem was that their names were not on the flight manifest, which was pointed out by the Indian officials, but they claimed it was a bureaucratic error on the part of the airlines, which they quickly got rectified.

With stamps of having entered India legally on their passport, the trio took a Pakistan International Airlines's flight to Karachi that was to depart at around 9.35 in the morning, and without a second glance they were able to smuggle themselves out of the country. The trio hopped from Karachi to Iran and eventually found their way to London.

Somewhere along their return, McLister either grew a conscience or became squeamish about the work Philby had him doing. The first opportunity he got he abandoned his companions and made a beeline for the Swiss Embassy. Once inside, he contacted the Interpol, and the first thing he revealed was that Philby was none other than India's most wanted infamous smuggler Daniel Hailey Walcott Jr.

With barely any time to lick its wounds, the Indian government was left red-faced again by another escape by India's Public Enemy Number One.

Meanwhile, the news of the plane landing in Murud was creating a stir abroad. Indian policemen were sent to London to investigate this curious incident and a mystery shrouded the entire episode. In the Parliament, the socialists used the events as ammo, alleging that India, which was once seen as the land of rich civilization, had been reduced to the land of get-rich-quick schemes for smugglers.

Time magazine, in an article on Walcott, described India as the 'world's richest market for smugglers'[6]. And Walcott and Donze made the most of it till they were caught two months

---

[6]'The Good Bad Man', *Time*, 2 November 1966, vol. 87 Issue 6, pg. 36

later in August. But that's not where the story ends. They were tried in what became one of the most thrilling cases involving maps, documents, conspiracies, espionage and a five-year prison sentence.

two

Natwarlal

Mithilesh Kumar Srivastava, or Natwarlal, belonged to a rare breed of crooks called 'thought criminals'.[1] He did not need a gun or weapons to rob people of their hard-earned cash or stickup a shop. His expertise lay in vanishing not only from the scene of crime but also from jails all over the country. By 1987, India's greatest con man had escaped from prison 10 times, which included seven times in Uttar Pradesh (UP) alone!

He boasted that no prison in India could hold him and as long as there was a dishonest cop, he would always find a way to get out!

What is most impressive about the life, crimes and escapes of Natwarlal is how seamlessly it leaves the realm of facts and enters the sphere of myth.

---

[1] Pradeep Kapoor and Sanjay Kapoor, 'India's Houdini', *BLITZ*, 14 November 1987

A 50-YEAR-LONG CAREER OF CRIME

It takes something special for names of people or things to be turned into verbs. You need to be able to capture the public's imagination as a unique entity. In recent years, for example, you do not 'search the internet' for information, you merely 'google it'. If you are fearless, you are called Sher Khan and if you are a manipulative personality in public life, in all likelihood, you'll be called Natwarlal. It is a name that is still used as a sobriquet.[2]

Born in 1913 in Ruiga village in the Siwan district of Bihar, Mithilesh Kumar Srivasatava's origins are shrouded in as much mystery as his entire life. While certain accounts claim that he came from a plebeian background much like the rest of India, others claim that he belonged to a well-to-do, land-owning class. He was an exceptionally bright boy, with a knack for everything but math, although he had no interests in studies.[3] Every anti-hero deserves a fitting origin story, and Natwarlal, too, has his fair share: two.

After a tiff with his teacher, his father got a whiff of his insolence and beat him to a pulp. The next day, young Mithilesh disappeared.[4] The other story is that he discovered his ability to forge signatures when a family friend of his, who went only by his surname, 'Sahay', sent him to deposit some money at

---

[2] Ibid.

[3] Dilip Bobb, Hoshi Jal, Farzand Ahmed, Lalitha Subramaniam. 'Natwarlal: Elusive King of Con', *India Today*, 15 August 1980, https://www.indiatoday.in/magazine/crime/story/19800815-natwarlal-a-con-man-par-excellence-a-master-forger-a-escape-artist-to-rival-houdini-821356-2014-01-27, last accessed on 6 November 2019

[4] Pradeep Kapoor and Sanjay Kapoor, 'India's Houdini', *BLITZ*, 14 November 1987

the bank. Srivastava copied Sahay's signature and discovered his ability to forge flawlessly. Over a period of time, he withdrew over ₹1,000 from the account. On being discovered, he disappeared.[5]

While both stories are different, they have one commonality—the disappearance of Mithilesh Srivastava and the emergence of Natwarlal. A move he would perfect in the years to come. This was a move he had used to his advantage in constantly escaping from prison or conning his way to freedom.

In 1932, he left Patna and made his way to Calcutta (now Kolkata), where he enrolled at Calcutta University in the bachelor's programme in Commerce. How he managed to gain admission is a mystery. It was in Calcutta that Natwarlal charted a path that brought him both notoriety and fame for the next 40 years. Over the next five years, he began work on his dubious activities. Natwarlal applied for jobs as a private tutor to many rich families, with reference letters from known people, substantiating his claim at being a great tutor. Where he got these letters from still remains a mystery. A share market broker, Seth Keshav Ram, hired him. A year later, young Natwarlal asked for a hike, but the seth refused to give him one. Furious, Natwarlal quit the job and through dubious credentials again, was appointed the principal of Shri Sanatan Dharam High School, where the seth's children studied. Once he secured the job, he began plotting his revenge. Keshav Ram, for some reason, was in the need of cotton and there was a paucity of

---

[5]Dilip Bobb, Hoshi Jal, Farzand Ahmed and Lalitha Subramaniam. 'Natwarlal: Elusive King of Con', *India Today*, 15 August 1980, https://www.indiatoday.in/magazine/crime/story/19800815-natwarlal-a-con-man-par-excellence-a-master-forger-a-escape-artist-to-rival-houdini-821356-2014-01-27, last accessed on 6 November 2019

cotton and cloth in the city. He convinced Seth Keshav Ram that his brother was bringing bales of cloth to Bombay and he would get them a good deal. They travelled to Bombay. Unware of Natwarlal's intentions, Keshav Ram sent him with the money to Bombay along with his munim, or accountant, to clinch the deal.

As this was Natwarlal's first trip to the western metropolis, he checked into the Stiffles Hotel, along with the accountant. Leaving the agent of the seth behind, he went around the city, acquainting himself with trading centres and the topography of the place.[6] He built up a story for the munim, one that painted the streets of Bombay as a dangerous place with gangs and tough cops who would not think twice before cutting someone up or putting them behind bars. The next day, the munim handed over the ₹4 lakh to Natwarlal, which he had to take to Kohinoor Mills, ostensibly to finalize the deal. It is unclear whether the seth's agent waited outside or at the hotel, but what is a fact is that Natwarlal took the money and disappeared through the back door.[7]

The munim went back to the seth and apprised him of what had happened. Meanwhile, Natwarlal went back home to his father and gave him ₹1 lakh, telling him that he had become a shareholder in a very big company in Calcutta. After spending a few days at home, he made his way back to Calcutta, where he was tracked down by Keshav Ram's men. On being found, Natwarlal was threatened with death and had only four days to return the money. He went to the police station and revealed the details of the various illegal operations run by his former

---

[6]Ibid.
[7]Ibid.

employer to the cops, who arrested Seth Keshav Ram and his men. The seth was not going down alone; he managed to get Natwarlal arrested too, who ended up spending only 14 months in jail and disappeared again. This time, he made his way to Madras (now Chennai), but not for long. There is only one incident registered to him in the southern city.[8]

There are various points in time when Natwarlal surfaced, like a little blip that appears and vanishes before you realize it. For example, in 1937, he came under the Calcutta police's scanner when he was caught selling iron joints that were kept on Metcalfe Street in Calcutta. He was accosted, arrested and imprisoned for a period of six months. History is replete with the instances of people who have been at the receiving end of the impeccable forgery and conning skills of Natwarlal.

In 1953, he and a toy-store dealer, Darashaw P. Dubash, were charged with encashing a cheque, fully knowing that it was forged. Dubash was supposed to receive a large sum of money from a certain Hirjibhai. The cheque in question was lost on the way to the toy-store dealer from Trivandrum (now Thiruvananthapuram), and Natwarlal was enlisted to forge the endorsement and the money was transferred to the account. Dubash claimed that he had received the amount from Hirjibhai, who did not have an account and had paid him the amount after receiving the receipt. The jury found them not guilty and they were acquitted.[9]

This was but the first of hundreds of crimes Mithilesh Kumar Srivastava, aka Natwarlal, would commit in a career

---

[8]Ibid.
[9]Staff Reporters, 'Jail Terms for Forgery Confirmed on Appeal', *The Times of India* (1861–current), 15 January 1975

that spanned over five decades and ended when he passed away at the age of 96.

JAILBREAKS

Indeed the Indian Penal Code's (IPC's) Section 420 (cheating and dishonesty) dogged his life, as well as a never-ending game of cat and mouse. Throughout his life, the police wanted to put him behind bars, but he always managed to be one step ahead.

His record of jailbreaks made him the legend that he is today. He was arrested by the police on many an occasion and was imprisoned under sections such as 420, 467, 463, 120-B of the IPC relating to criminal conspiracy and forgery, but never for too long.

The first time his disappearance caused a stir was in 1953, when, in the midst of the trial in the Punjab National Bank (PNB) cheating case, he escaped from the custody of the police. Before that, according to the crime intelligence gazette of the UP police, he had also disappeared from the judicial lock-up in Delhi.

In 1957, he executed his most brilliant escape. Natwarlal was arrested in Meerut on charges of cheating and he had interned at Lucknow Jail a year earlier. During this time, he had a close associate who went by his surname, 'Kapoor'. This associate was tasked with only one job: to bring gifts for the jailor, Abdul Rehman Khan. Kapoor would do just that. He regularly brought all types of presents for Khan, who was slowly won over. Once the jailor softened, Natwarlal offered him a sum of ₹5 lakh on a condition that he would be allowed to escape.[10]

---

[10]Pradeep Kapoor and Sanjay Kapoor, 'India's Houdini', *BLITZ*, 14 November 1987

Kapoor played the role of the intermediary and the jailor fell for the bait, hook, line and sinker. On the agreed day, Kapoor came with the money and Khan went through the box full of currency notes to his satisfaction. As promised, he sent a superintendent's uniform to Natwarlal's cell. Natwarlal promptly wore it and leisurely sauntered out of the prison and disappeared into a waiting car.

After Natwarlal disappeared, an excited Khan examined his booty and found to his horror that only the top layer in the box contained genuine currency notes—underneath were merely pieces of paper! What happened next has continued to puzzle crime experts to this day, the box with the money suddenly caught fire and the money was set ablaze. This final trick of the con man sent Khan's hope up in smoke.

In UP alone, Natwarlal had been convicted in 20 cases. There is very little information on the man and his enigmatic life. Strangely, very few accounts have survived the test of time. In 1956, there was a flood in Lucknow in which all his files were washed away. The Bihar police only have records detailing his crimes till the age of 44.

He used to prey on people's weaknesses, and the vice he exploited the most was greed.

After successfully duping Khan, Natwarlal was tracked, rearrested and brought back to Lucknow Jail almost immediately. His recapture and return to the prison saved the police some embarrassment, but the entire prison staff was suspended following his escape. However, the respite of the jail authorities was only short-lived, as Natwarlal found another way out of the prison and waltzed out again, leaving the police licking its wounds.

Natwarlal had perfected the technique that he had first

adopted in Lucknow Jail and employed it again and again—the art of vanishing. His modus operandi was largely the same for nearly five decades. He would convince jail guards that someone was waiting or some money was to be gotten, and they would get a cut, and when the moment was right, he would give them the slip.

Another confirmed instance is from Kakinada Sub-jail in Andhra Pradesh. It was this manipulation of policemen that stood him in good stead in his commission of crimes.[11]

ASSISTANTS

Contrary to popular belief that Natwarlal operated alone, he was always aided by accomplices, who were mostly attractive women (more specifically, prostitutes). The early part of his career was devoted to drugging them and stealing their valuables. However, he changed tact and enlisted their help in his conning and forging. In 1956, Khurshid Fatimam, alias Afsar Zamini, a prostitute, used to masquerade as his wife, and was used as a decoy to lure rich men in his trap.

Natwarlal mostly dealt with bogus railway receipts, which came in handy while taking delivery of goods from godowns. According to one estimate from 1963, he had managed to swing a delivery of items worth ₹1 crore. The money was generally stashed away in some bank under fake names. Natwarlal was reportedly earning almost ₹3 lakh per year as interest on dubious bank deposits alone.

In 1977/78, he cheated L.N. Mittal of Muzaffarnagar using the 'railway-receipt trick'. He would pretend to be interested in

---

[11] Ibid.

buying goods and pay small amounts to the traders, but move them on the other end at much larger sums. However, his plan was not squeaky clean and he was soon caught.[12]

In 1979, while lodged in a Bombay prison, Natwarlal said that he had developed a medical condition and had to be admitted to J.J. Hospital. One evening, while in the hospital, he convinced the constable guarding him to take him to Taj Hotel, where he had a friend waiting to give him a large amount of money. He convinced the constable that if he allowed him to go, he would be happy to share a cut of the bounty. Once they reached the hotel, he told the constable to wait downstairs in the lobby till he came back with the money. The constable waited for half an hour before realizing that things had taken a wrong turn. No one saw Natwarlal for several years after that.[13]

The police tried to track down a woman and two grown-up children who often went to meet him in prison, but they were nowhere to be found either.

ONE FINAL ACT

After missing in action for nearly seven years, the bug to do something big began to bite him again. One last scheme before he retired. Once he had a plan in his head, he could not stop

---

[12] Dilip Bobb, Hoshi Jal, Farzand Ahmed, Lalitha Subramaniam, 'Natwarlal: Elusive King of Con', *India Today*, 15 August 1980, https://www.indiatoday.in/magazine/crime/story/19800815-natwarlal-a-con-man-par-excellence-a-master-forger-a-escape-artist-to-rival-houdini-821356-2014-01-27, last accessed on 6 November 2019

[13] Staff Reporter, 'Undertrial Taken by Cop to Taj Hotel, Escapes', *The Times of India* (1861–current), 30 June 1980

himself. Mithilesh Kumar Srivastava re-emerged with a clear agenda: to concentrate only on watch dealers. In a matter of six months, he had duped almost a dozen watch dealers in Kanpur, Delhi and Varanasi.

His plan was simple. He found a few gullible printers, with whom he printed bogus chequebooks. These were used liberally all over the country to dupe watch sellers. In Delhi, he introduced himself as an assistant to the then finance minister, Narayan Dutt Tiwari, and claimed that the Indian National Congress (INC) (I) was having a function where watches were to be presented to all the delegates. On another occasion, he assumed the role of the personal secretary of the then finance minister, V.P. Singh, and convinced shopkeepers that his son was getting married, and they needed the watches as presents. He took up various aliases and spun the same yarn. In Delhi, he lifted as many as 97 watches from a shop, and in Kanpur, he walked away with jewellery worth ₹1.5 lakh.[14]

His cheating finally caught up with him and he was nabbed in Varanasi. True to his wont, he kept fooling the police officials.

The story of his arrest in 1987 is as ridiculous as the crimes he committed. When taken to the police station in Varanasi, he was taken in for processing. The police inspector on duty sent a message to his counterpart in the Criminal Investigation Department in Patna asking for the details of an Ambika Pandey, the alias he was going by. As they waited for the report to come back from Patna, the inspector continued to ask him who he was and Natwarlal, in his theatrical fashion, promised to tell him who he was if and only if he was not disturbed. Befuddled,

---

[14]Pradeep Kapoor and Sanjay Kapoor, 'India's Houdini', *BLITZ*, 14 November 1987

the police officer went away and waited for the response. What the officer on duty did not realize was that the unobtrusive, pot-bellied, innocuous-looking old man in his custody was none other than Natwarlal, the legendary con man.

In the interim, the police fanned out its search for any information. They finally struck a patch of good luck when his accomplices—the printers—were caught in Allahabad. Meanwhile, the master criminal was losing patience, and at six in the evening, on 1 November, he blew the lid and told the inspector that he was none other than the 'famous' Natwarlal— the man that everyone thought was dead. At 73, he was still pulling off more crimes than others could even dream of. He begun talking about his cases to the police officers, regaling them with all the old stories of cons, crimes and forgeries he had committed, fully aware that what he was saying in custody could not be used against him in court.[15]

In 1991, Natwarlal escaped again. He was being led to the railway station in a wheelchair as he had claimed to be infirm. At the station, he asked the constable to get him something, and when the officer left, he got up and walked the other way.[16]

DEATH

It is unclear whether Natwarlal died in 1996 or 2009. In 1996, his brother claimed that he was dead and got all the cases against

---

[15] Raj Chengappa, 'The Life and Crimes of a Master Criminal Natwarlal', *India Today*, 30 November 1987, https://www.indiatoday.in/magazine/special-report/story/19871130-the-life-and-crimes-of-a-master-criminal-natwarlal-799579-1987-11-30, last accessed on 6 November 2019

[16] N.K. Singh, 'Legendary Master-Criminal Natwarlal Unrepentant', 30 June 1991, *India Today*

him dismissed, claiming to have cremated the body. In 2009, his lawyer came to the local administration and informed them of the demise of Mithilesh Kumar Srivastava. The officers were scratching their heads wondering how a man who had died 13 years ago could die again.

Much like most other aspects of his life, it was difficult to separate the truth from the myth, the fact from the fiction. But what contributed to the myth or the legend was his Robin Hood-esque actions. Reportedly he had said that his interests lay in duping big-moneyed men off ₹50,000[17] and above at a time, and distributing it amongst the poor. Maybe that's why even a suggestion was made to set up a statue of the criminal in his village, which is also the hometown of Dr Rajendra Prasad, the first president of India.

---

[17] Ratnakar Tripathy, 'Natwarlal: A Wodehousian Criminal', The Times of India Research Bureau, *The Times of India* (1861–current), 1 July 1991

three

Charles Sobhraj:
How to Run a Prison and Walk Out of It

6 APRIL 1986

Madhukar Baburao Zende had reached Goa four days ago. He had been observing the two men whom he knew to be the escapee and his accomplice. That afternoon, Zende sauntered up to the table where the two men—one distinctly Asian and the other Caucasian—sat in O' Coquiero, an upscale restaurant in Goa, and said, 'Hello, Charles. How are you?'

A little less than a month ago, on 16 March 1986, Charles Sobhraj, one of the most infamous serial killers in the world, had walked out of New Delhi's Tihar Jail and vanished.[1]

The manhunt had been on for two weeks. All possible leads were being followed up on. International help had been requested and a red alert had been sent to the Interpol. The government was under the scanner; the laxity and complicit

---

[1] Staff Reporter, 'Blow by Blow', *The Times of India*, 8 April 1986

nature of the 'great' escape demanded a closer look at the urgent need for reforming the functioning of Tihar. One by one, six other escapees found their way back into the hands of the police, and a tip-off by Ajai Singh, one of the convicts who had escaped with Sobhraj, had led the Special Team to Goa.

The response from the man believed to be Charles Sobhraj was cool, calm and firm. 'Are you crazy? You must be mad!' Zende was only too familiar with this dance and he explained how, 15 years ago, it was he who had nearly apprehended him in Bombay. Out of nowhere, Sobhraj pulled out a pistol—a Llama. Unfortunately for him, it was no match for Zende and the 10 police officers stationed strategically around the restaurant. Sobhraj was quickly disarmed.

Less than a month later, he walked out of Tihar, where he had celebrated his faux birthday on the afternoon of 16 March 1986. Sobhraj was going right back to jail on his 'real' 42nd birthday.

16 MARCH 1986: THE PARTY

Two men stepped into a white Ambassador outside their hotel in Connaught Place, Delhi. It was around 11 o'clock in the morning and they made their way to the Tihar Jail complex, Asia's largest penitentiary. It was a Sunday and they were headed to celebrate Charles Sobhraj's birthday. They were carrying with them an assortment of sweets, including fruit custard, pedhas and also grapes. At the gate of Jail 3 of Tihar, two guards belonging to the Tamil Nadu Special Police and warder Ram Chander were waiting along with a foreigner, who was later identified as David Hallman. Along with them was an Indian gentleman in a khaki outfit, who was suspected to be either Raju Bhatnagar, the famous dacoit or Ajay Chowdhury, Sobhraj's elusive second in command.[2]

At the gate, they informed that they had come to celebrate Charles saab's birthday and were immediately let in. In Tihar, matters related to 'permissions were not sought but taken'.[3] When they entered, they found the assistant superintendent, S.R. Yadav, lost in conversation with the man they had come to meet. In a matter of 20 minutes, the group sped away in the white car only pausing to leave an unconscious warder Anand Prakash in the middle of the road, gagged and bound.[4]

When the police officials reached the room where the party was held, they found that crisp new 50-rupee notes had been tucked into the jail officials' breast pockets. As the officers regained consciousness, they realized what had happened. Charles Sobhraj had sauntered out of jail, proving to the world that he was no ordinary criminal, but more importantly proving something he had been saying for years—if he truly wanted to escape, there was nothing stopping him.

PREPARATIONS

A few days before the dreaded escape, a cat was found unconscious in the gardens of Jail 3 of Tihar. On the first day, it lay fast asleep; warders and prisoners alike could not tell why it would not wake up or move. By the third day, still weak, it began to walk around. Little did anyone know that the man who had perfected the 'drug-rob-kill' method was just trying his hand

---

[2]Dibang, 'Jail Break!' *The Illustrated Weekly of India*, 30 March 1986
[3]Ibid.
[4]Ibid.

with the sedative that had been passed to him from outside.[5]

There was an uninterrupted channel of exchange, communications and privileges for the man who had notoriously picked up several identities in the decade-long career as a con man and murderer.

Cells 8 and 9 were shared by two other convicts, Ajai Singh and Laxmi Narain (two other convicts who escaped), respectively. There was a kitchen where the meal for the party was prepared.[6] Since this discovery, no cooking has been allowed in Tihar.

Richard Neville and Julie Clarke's book, *The Life and Crimes of Charles Sobhraj: On the Trail of the Serpent*, published in 1979, that details the complicated, tortured and devious journey of the criminal mastermind, was in many ways prescient: 'It will be on one of those lazy tropical afternoons when the interest in the case has waned, and the flies buzz and the guards doze in the heat, that Charles Sobhraj will make his move.'

He did indeed wait, making his move only when he knew that he had absolute control and power—his psychological games had yielded their results—and the consequences of the move would benefit him, and only him.

SUPER CRIME SYNDROME

In 1980, a case filed by Rakesh Kaushik, a lifer, was heard in the Supreme Court of India. Kaushik claimed that within the walls of Tihar Central Jail ran an internal syndicate that spread

---

[5] Shekhar Gupta, 'Charles Sobhraj's Escape from Tihar Jail Sets Off One of the Biggest Manhunts in India', *India Today*, 15 April 1986
[6] Press Trust of India, 'Sobhraj's Fun Filled Days in Tihar', 21 March 1986

'...terror and horror, physical and psychic, let loose on him and other jail-mates', but this was done by a 'crypto criminal combination' of senior jail officials and influential prisoners, 'thereby making the prison life within that walled world such a trauma and torment [that] the law never meant under the sentence suffered at the hands of the court'. At the centre of this 'combination' was Charles Sobhraj.[7]

He had almost every conceivable luxury in his cell in Tihar. He had a 14-inch television, a cassette player and innumerable cassettes. The police had refused to disclose what were on the tapes, but it was pretty clear what they had found.[8]

It was through the cunning use of technology— surreptitiously hidden recorders and microphones—and free legal help that 'The Serpent', a nickname for Sobhraj, gained control of the prison. He would record junior officials in the prison speaking ill of higher authorities and build up an entire archive of such recordings of exchanges, bribes and other incriminating stuffs. The fact that no one tried to take or snatch them was a testament to his power.[9]

In a conversation with an official who worked at Tihar in the '80s, Charles used the law and technology to his advantage. In 1978/79, he filed a petition against his 'bar fetters or manacles' with Sunil Batra, who was Delhi's first bank robber and part of Sobhraj's coterie, and got them removed. He helped all those in his coterie with their cases; he had help from Sneha Sangar,

---

[7] Rakesh Kaushik vs B.L. Vig and Ors, Supreme Court of India, 30 April 1980
[8] Dibang, 'Jail Break!' *The Illustrated Weekly of India*, 30 March 1986
[9] Sunil Batra vs Delhi Admininstration and Ors. and Charles Gurumukh Sobhraj. State of Delhi, 1979

a young female lawyer who helped him draft his cases.[10] His knowledge of the law and a steady flow of money won him the trust of a group of hardened criminals. Sobhraj took David Hallman, a narcotics smuggler, under his protection and assisted Raju Bhatnagar, a serial kidnapper, to get bail, which the dacoit immediately jumped.[11]

Jails offered him a unique opportunity—he had a steady stream of new recruits, the best networks and gangs. This small coterie or clique exerted absolute influence and brought the system under their control.[12] His clique included Raju Bhatnagar, Sunil Batra and Ajai Singh Choudhary, amongst several others. This influence was limited to those around him, but extended to the officials in the prison too. For example, when Bhatnagar wanted to change his prison cell to Sobhraj's, no questions were asked and it was done. According to a rumour, when Giani Zail Singh, the then home minister, visited Tihar, he found that Sobhraj was not in his cell but elsewhere. This was the power exerted by Sobhraj in prison.[13]

In his confession, one of the six who escaped from Tihar with Sobhraj, Bhola Ram, another criminal, revealed that it was Raju Bhatnagar who had orchestrated the entire escape. Even Hallman was a narcotics smuggler who was out on bail largely due to the resources and connections of Sobhraj.

---

[10]Shekhar Gupta, 'Charles Sobhraj's Escape from Tihar Jail Sets Off One of the Biggest Manhunts in India', *India Today*, 15 April 1986

[11]Dibang, 'Jail Break!' *The Illustrated Weekly of India*, 30 March 1986

[12]Press Trust of India, 'Probe Tihar Jail Racket Orders Supreme Court', 30 April 1980

[13]Dibang, 'Jail Break!' *The Illustrated Weekly of India*, 30 March 1986

OF GRAPES, CUSTARD AND PEDHAS

The party had begun. An elaborate feast was laid out on the table. Sobhraj moved out of the superintendent's room to bring two more inmates and in a matter of minutes came back with Laxmi Narain and Brijmohan. In this time, Warder Anand Prakash, Assistant Superintendent Yadav, Warder Ram Chander and two Tamil Nadu Special constables, along with two other lifers, had begun gobbling up the custard, pedhas and grapes. The sedative hit them immediately and they felt drowsy.[14]

Sobhraj re-entered the room with two other inmates and signaled Hallman and Bhatnagar to initiate the second part of the plan.[15] As the police officers and the prisoners began to collapse, the two tied their arms and legs, taped their mouths and pushed them in a corner. Meanwhile, Yadav, half-lucid, tried to make a lunge, rather unsuccessfully, at the group. He was easily subdued and tied down with the rest.

All of them, but for Warder Prakash, were left behind. Holding his unconscious body up, they guided Prakash to the car. They made him sit on the side where the guards stood at the main gate and drove out. The unconscious warder waved at the guards and the white Ambassador was off. Ten minutes later, they stopped on the side of the road, left the drugged warder there and drove off into the distance.

---

[14]Ibid.
[15]Ibid.

3.00 P.M.

As Warder Prakash gained consciousness,[16] he found himself lying flat, gagged and bound, on the side of the road 10 minutes away from Tihar. He had vivid memories of being led past the deodhi—the area that people have to cross at times of arrival and departure—to the white Ambassador that stood waiting and being made to sit next to Sobhraj.[17] What had started off as a birthday celebration in the office of Assistant Superintendent Yadav had officially turned into a nightmare of epic proportions.

A helpful auto driver who was driving from the other side spotted the officer, freed him and then dropped him to Tihar. Prakash ran to the office and picked up the phone to call his superior.

It was late afternoon when the phone rang. V.D. Pushkarna, the deputy superintendent of Tihar's Jail 3, was in his office. He reached for the receiver and heard the frantic voice of Prakash. The phone call made things clear. Charles Gurmukh Sobhraj, the most notorious criminal that the region and perhaps the country had ever seen, had just walked out of the gates of the jail, where he had spent close to a decade.

Unknown to him at that point was that in a few weeks' time, images of him being led to court would be splashed all over the newspapers, a curse as his colleagues say, still follows him today. But on that March afternoon in 1986, it was Pushkarna's turn to pick up the phone and call the police.

---

[16] This is contested. According to Prakash, he never left Tihar and was drugged, much like everybody else.

[17] Dibang, 'Jail Break!' *The Illustrated Weekly of India*, 30 March 1986

In a matter of less than an hour, Ved Marwah, the commissioner of Delhi, put the state on high alert. Checkpoints and barricades were immediately set up in all quarters of the city. Airports were put on high-security alerts and monitored. After all, no ordinary man had walked out of Tihar Jail that afternoon; it was Mr Evil himself.

Sunil Gupta, who retired as the press officer of Tihar, was watching television. He was then the Deputy Superintendent of Police and was posted in the jail in 1986. He remembers vividly, 'It was a Sunday and I was sitting at home watching a movie, which was suddenly interrupted. The news announcer looked and said that Charles Sobhraj, the notorious criminal mastermind wanted in over four continents, had escaped from Tihar Central Jail and was at large.'

Tension gripped the city, and all resources and personnel were called back. Gupta's Sunday, too, was cut short, and he made his way to the prison.

Little by little, information began to trickle in. According to an early report, immediately after the escape, an unidentified man had tried to tell the Tamil Nadu Special Police at the main gate what had happened and that they should raise an alarm, but it was lost in translation!

Everyone in Delhi's administration ran to Tihar, where they found the drugged and dazed police officers. All of them had crisp new 50-rupee notes tucked into their pockets. The mutterings of an inside job and help began doing the rounds immediately. Over the next week, several police officers, including Pushkarna, were taken to jail.[18]

In the interim, barricades, security details and checkposts were set up, but it was too late. The border of Haryana is only 10 km from Tihar and that was where the white Ambassador headed. Over the next few days, the news was rife with speculation. *Where would Sobhraj go?* News media from every corner of the globe converged in New Delhi, poring over every detail of the case, and told the world the story of the sleeping serpent who slid away from captivity.

After another alleged escape, all the prisoners were counted. The same happened in the late afternoon of the 16th. After the counting, they found that, in addition to the obvious missing inmate, five others, too, had escaped—Laxmi Narain, Brijmohan, Bhola Ram, Dinesh Kumar and Ajai Singh.

OF SEARCHES, NEXUS AND ARRESTS

In the aftermath of the escape, several prison officers were arrested on charges of conniving with an international criminal. S.D. Lakhar, a senior official of the Delhi administration, was made in-charge of finding out about the situation in the jail. It was alleged that there was gross violation of the jail manual. The prisoner, according to the report, was permitted to engage in long meetings with visitors who were allowed into the deodhi, and were given privacy and secrecy. The privileges given to Sobhraj amounted to sheer negligence. Yadav and Pushkarna were immediately arrested on the grounds of conniving with a criminal. According to a committee set up by H.L. Kapur,

---

[18]'Jail Staff Helped Sobhraj Escape', The Times of India News Service, 8 June 1986

the Lt Governor of Delhi, the two police officers had ignored the police manual and given a free hand to Sobhraj. However, Pushkarna's life had another twist waiting for him.[19]

Sobhraj's modus operandi always involved a woman. There were several with whom he was in touch with when he was with Sneha Sangar, a young law graduate student from Delhi University. She was found in her hometown of Lalitpur, near Jhansi, UP. However, she was immediately arrested for involvement in the conspiracy. Another man, Daljeet Singh Bhalla, a 31-year-old philosophy and religion student from San Francisco, was picked up at an upscale restaurant in New Delhi. It was alleged that Rajinder Singh Sethia, the world's biggest bankrupt who was serving time in jail for a multimillion-dollar financial swindle,[20] funded the escape and had routed the money through his nephew, Bhalla. It was alleged by Sangar that Sethia had even financed the legal fees for Bhatnagar's case and was very close to Sobhraj.[21]

All these were allegations and did not amount to much.

UNRAVELLING

The case of escape began unravelling itself quite quickly. Dinesh Kumar, one of the escapees, returned to custody almost immediately. He claimed that he was also drugged and walked out of the jail behind the Ambassador. According to him, he wasn't spotted as he was wearing regular clothes. His prison

---

[19] Ibid.
[20] Press Trust of India, 'Sobhraj-Sethia Nexus Alleged', 29 March 1986
[21] Shekhar Gupta, 'Charles Sobhraj's Escape from Tihar Jail Sets Off One of the Biggest Manhunts in India', *India Today*, 15 April 1986

clothes were in the laundry, which is done on Sundays in Tihar. He was dropped off at Chandni Chowk and he walked to the Delhi railway station, where he encountered a coolie to whom he narrated the entire story of his escape. The gentleman, after hearing his entire story, told him to return to the jail and turn himself in and that's what Dinesh did.

A week later, Bhola Ram was caught in Gwalior, and then one by one the pieces began to fall together.

Sobhraj languished in Tihar for another 10 years and was released in 1997. He left India and made his way to France, where for the next seven years he lived life like a celebrity, charging exorbitant amounts for interviews and public appearances. However, in 2003, he was sighted in Kathmandu and arrested by the Nepali police, who sentenced him to life imprisonment for the murder of two tourists.[22] Since 2004, he has been interned in Nepal, serving a life sentence. No matter his term, one thing remains certain—whatever Sobhraj does is calculated and planned, never impulsive.

---

[22]'Nepal Court Convicts "Bikini Killer" Charles Sobhraj of Second Murder', *BBC News*, 18 September 2014, https://www.bbc.com/news/world-asia-29261120, last accessed on 6 November 2019

four

Sukur Narayan Bakhia: Hide-and-Seek

It had been a roller coaster of a week for Sukur Narayan Bakhia. The police had picked him up on 11 September 1974, on charges that he vehemently disagreed with and opposed. There was little doubt in the minds of the arresting officers that the man they had picked up was a notorious smuggler. However, Bakhia claimed that he had never seen a bar of gold in his life, and that he was *not* a smuggler. Moreover, if they had just given him the chance, he would have joined in their fight against the scum.[1]

His downfall was a poorly executed money-laundering exercise involving 22 very influential people and a crossword puzzle.

During the 1960s, '70s and '80s, India and its coastline

---

[1]Staff Reporter, 'Prove Guilt: Bakhia', *The Times of India* (1861–current), 18 September 1974

were in the tight grips of three of the biggest smugglers in South Asia, perhaps even bigger than the Colombian drug lord, Pablo Escobar. Haji Mastan, Yusuf Patel and Sukur Narayan Bakhia smuggled in watches, gold and other contraband and by selling them in black ran a parallel market. In today's liberalized economic environment, would these men have been criminals? Maybe not, as half of their enterprise would have been legitimate!

A week after he was arrested on 11 September 1974, the same court that issued his warrant gave him respite by allowing him to furnish bail. Immediately after being arrested, he suffered a heart attack—a man so pure of heart could not take the pressures of being accused of being a smuggler. He was immediately sent to a nursing home in Bombay. And, a day later, he received bail and lay recovering at Dr Bacha's Memorial Belle Vue Nursing Home in Marine Lines.

Following the doctor's strict instructions of not straining himself, Bakhia dictated a letter to his lawyer, S. Venkateswaran, who assiduously penned it down and mailed it to the then union minister of state for finance, K.R. Ganesh. In the letter, Bakhia dissuaded the authorities from believing in the baseless accusation made by the enforcement authorities and did nothing more to sully his image. He claimed he was not the Sukur Narayan Bakhia they were looking for, and that there was little or no basis to their allegations. He further claimed that the moment he recovered from the heart attack that left him immobilized, he would help the government in stopping the scourge of smuggling.[2]

The next day, however, the government did something that

---

[2]Ibid.

Bakhia and several others like him did not want or expect. It extended the purview of the Maintenance of Internal Security Act (MISA) to cover acts of smuggling and indefinitely held Bakhia.

Sukur Narayan Bakhia was a short man, all of 5'4", but his height was no measure of the power he wielded. Growing up in the coastal territory of Daman, he was born to a family of fishermen. During his growing-up years, he lived a life of penury. As a young man, he began working in the lower rungs of the mafia, ferrying goods in and out under the eyes of the state. Despite all the money he would go on to make over his life, living in a large mansion in Daman, he always maintained that he was a middle-class man, making money off rented properties. He paid ₹283 in taxes in 1979–80 and ₹480 in 1980–81.[3]

This man living in penury was affectionately called Ganpati, or Mafia Don. The first recorded arrest of Bakhia was in 1962, when the police nabbed him for smuggling a small amount of contraband goods. The leader of the gang he worked for paid his bail and he was released. He was a slave to his ambition, and it did not take Bakhia very long to set his eyes on the bigger prize—his own smuggling enterprises. It was a modest start, with him picking up watches from dhows, small boats used in

---

[3]Ramesh Menon, 'The Return of Bakhia', *India Today*, 15 August 1982, https://www.indiatoday.in/magazine/indiascope/story/19820815-after-breaking-out-of-fort-aguada-jail-sukur-naran-bakhia-turns-himself-in-772097-2013-10-05, last accessed on 29 January 2020

the Arabian Sea for transport and selling them to a Goan sailor named Joseph.[4]

It was just a matter of time before the smuggler made a name for himself and his operations grew manifold. His first order of business was to set up a base of operations in Dubai and then from there to expand his interests to Singapore and finally, Hong Kong. He made money through several channels. Other than smuggling, he dipped his toes in the world of hawala transactions and racketeering and eventually real estate too. But he always continued to smuggle copious amounts of gold and contraband goods into the country. A boat named Jalaram Vishwas was intercepted by INS Brahmaputra on its way to Daman on 16 February 1971. The coastguard boarded the ship and searched it thoroughly. The crew, when interrogated, revealed that right before the officials had boarded, they had thrown large amounts of gold—worth almost ₹5 lakh—overboard. Over the next three days, the ship was kept afloat while the divers went down and recovered the gold from the seabed. In the meanwhile, the crew of the dhow was also repeatedly interrogated, but the question they needed an answer to was *who* did they work for. Atham Fakir, the owner of the boat, finally broke down and blurted out that he was to head towards Daman, where once he reached close enough to the coast, he would signal the men of a certain S.N. Bakhia, who would come and offload the vessel.[5]

---

[4] Asoka Raina, 'The Don of Daman', *India Today*, 15 May 1982, https://www.indiatoday.in/magazine/crime/story/19820515-underworld-don-sukur-naran-bakhia-finally-arrested-by-custom-officials-in-daman-771799-2013-10-16, last accessed on 29 January 2020

[5] K.S. Dilipsinhji, Member (T), Sukar Naran vs Collector of Customs and Central…on 29 August 1986

These men were nothing more than errand boys, doing Bakhia's bidding; pawns in an international smuggling ring of which he was the centre. Hidden behind layers and layers of operatives, companies and people, it was almost impossible to pin him down. Whenever the police got close, he mustered up a battery of lawyers.

The boat captain's confession led the customs officials to Bakhia's doorstep, who, to protect himself, deployed all the resources he could to clear his name. In his mind, his defence was simple. As there was no physical evidence tying him to the ship or its cargo, his name was not part of the manifest; he could at best be charged as a co-conspirator. Even the raid at his house led to nothing. The narrative built by his lawyers did not convince the judge and they slapped a fine of ₹10 lakh on him. Despite this setback, the mafia don did not stop his operation, as he was under a carefully built protection system. The don was very clear about the benefits that would accrue with the proximity to political power; several family members were fielded as Members of Legislative Assembly in Goa and as MPs from Daman.[6] His family was allegedly close to several political parties and that would ensure protection during difficult times. However, these were still kinks in his armour.

In 1969, he began a complex operation, an ingenious scheme to convert black money into white. Through it, he could literally game the system. Bakhia, with the help of a man named Navin Patel, opened a crossword puzzle-making

---

[6]Asoka Raina, 'Bakhia Breaks Out', *India Today*, 30 June 1982, https://www.indiatoday.in/magazine/indiascope/story/19820630-smuggler-sukur-naran-bakhia-breaks-out-of-fort-aguada-prison-in-goa-771902-2013-10-08, last accessed on 29 January 2020

company in Daman and Gujarat that hosted competitions with prize money. The crossword was a puzzle called 'Sabd Bari Hai'. The scheme was simple. The prize money was to be tax-free and those who wanted to turn their unaccounted wealth into 'white money' had to get in touch with the office and they would be declared that week's winner. Numerous doctors, businessmen and several criminals made full use of this scheme. In the next four years, as the police worked overtime to crack the case, Patel turned against the smuggling kingpin and became a state's witness. For a good part of a decade, the police tried to pin down the smuggler in this case, but with little or no success.[7]

If the boat had put the officials on his scent in 1971, the crossword puzzle was his undoing in 1974, and by 1982, it was his avarice, his love for liquor and women that eventually triggered his fall.

The story of the contest between him and the authorities was a never-ending one. It invariably began with an accusation that was promptly denied and then devolved into a game of hide-and-seek.

However, Bakhia was a product of his time and the legal regime that imposed severe restrictions on the way people lived and worked. India was a closed economy, tightly bound by strict laws that controlled the inflow, exchange and hoarding of goods. Any violation was keenly observed and these factors motivated those who sent him to prison.

---

[7]Judge V. Bedarkar, Sukar Narayan Bakhia vs Income Tax on 6 August 1982, https://indiankanoon.org/doc/1061319/, last accessed on 29 January 2020

SMUGGLING

Right after the 1962 war with China, the then finance minister, Morarji Desai, prohibited gold futures in an attempt to control the outflow of foreign exchange. The decision to impose a strict control on gold ownership, a precious metal that lends weight to an economy, came as a shock to goldsmiths and the gold traders whose livelihoods came under serious threat.

Owning, handling and keeping gold beyond a certain weight was illegal. This decision was backed by the Conservation of Foreign Exchange and Prevention of Smuggling Activities Act (COFEPOSA), 1974, which gave the revenue, income tax and other finance-related departments teeth.

ESCAPE(S)

The past few years had been tumultuous for Bakhia, as he had to leave the country during and after the Emergency. He refused to give up smuggling even despite Jayaprakash Narayan asking all Indian smugglers to stop in the aftermath of the Emergency. His closeness with the INC was something he took for granted and thought it would give him political cover, but that was not the case.[8]

In May 1982, Bakhia's appetite for his vices got the better of him. He began to prey on young girls but made the folly of hunting in Daman. The family of the girl he had tried to act fresh with ratted out the entirety of Bakhia's operation to the authorities, who seized his incoming shipments and arrested

---

[8]Staff Correspondent, 'Two Top Goa Govt. Officials Replaced', *The Times of India* (1861–current), 6 June 1982

his son-in-law. What followed was a miraculous game of cat and mouse.[9]

The man, who had been on the run from the customs department for more than a decade, was finally caught after four months of painstaking sleuthing. The tip from the family had opened a pandora's box. Now, as the investigation began to take shape, the layers of secrecy and security that were required to arrest him were watertight. Police officers working on the case kept the facts of the investigation to themselves. Only a handful of cops knew what was happening, and when and where he would finally be caught. Bakhia was lodged at Fort Aguada Jail.

Bakhia began plotting his escape the moment he entered the prison. He had worked too hard to be put away with such ease and permanence. It only took him two months to free himself from within the walls of the jail.

According to a report by Ramakant Khalap of the Maharashtrawadi Gomantak Party, a regional political party from Goa, the smuggler enjoyed immense freedom and limitless perquisites inside the jail. Much to everyone's surprise, he had written that 'Sukur Bakhia seems happy',[10] and when he escaped from prison, Khalap went hammer and tongs against his political rivals, the INC (I), with a massive 'I told you so'.

After one of his jail visits, Khalap was of the opinion that the prison would not be able to hold Bakhia much longer. There was also growing evidence that the don had begun to spend lavishly

---

[9] Asoka Raina, 'The Don of Daman', *India Today*, 15 May 1982, https://www.indiatoday.in/magazine/crime/story/19820515-underworld-don-sukur-naran-bakhia-finally-arrested-by-custom-officials-in-daman-771799-2013-10-16, last accessed on 29 January 2020

[10] M.J. Kamalakar, 'Jailer Held Door Open for Bakhia', *The Times of India* (1861–current), 4 June 1982

in prison, giving out money to the jail officials. Favours and privileges can be bought in jail, even from the prison guards who are as impoverished, underpaid and desperate as the prisoners. The leader of the regional party was not wrong in assuming that there was collusion even in the Goa Assembly, and in the Parliament, there was a standoff. MPs wanted answers to how smugglers of repute were waltzing out of prison if there was no patronage. He had been a beneficiary of political patronage; his family was also linked to the INC from Daman to Goa.

The Bombay High Court, after one of his several pleas, said that there was little or no ground on which he could be detained. And the police and the customs department were not ready or willing to release him from custody just yet. The enforcement and customs authorities were afraid that once out, he would go right back to smuggling. As a remedy, they decided that Bakhia should be transferred to Gujarat and interned at a prison there. As the case proceeded in his time, the man known as Ganpati grew restless in prison. He even sent his brother-in-law, Haribhai Tandel, who was also a local politician, to request for his release.

On the morning of 29 May 1982, two police officers from the Gujarat State Police came with an arrest warrant in the name of Bakhia. When they reached the jail, they realized that they could not re-arrest Bakhia till the time he was released from prison.[11] A quick fix was sought. They rushed to the lieutenant governor, who signed the order on the night of the 29th. Then,

---

[11] Asoka Raina, 'Smuggler Sukur Naran Bakhia Breaks Out of Fort Aguada Prison in Goa', *India Today*, 30 June 1982, https://www.indiatoday.in/magazine/indiascope/story/19820630-smuggler-sukur-naran-bakhia-breaks-out-of-fort-aguada-prison-in-goa-771902-2013-10-08, last accessed on 29 January 2020

the police officers from Ahmedabad went to the jail, where the superintendent of the jail, S.U. Kamat, met them. They made Bakhia read the order, who claimed he could not read it due to poor light in the cell.

The next morning, they reached the gates of the jail but were not permitted to enter by Kamat. He flatly refused to let them in and said that Bakhia would be brought out to them.

The police officers waited, and few minutes turned to half an hour and then eventually an hour when they realized that Bakhia was not coming. The police officers were furious and made their way into the jail, and to their utter shock, found that Bakhia had fled from the backdoor as they had been waiting outside! It turned out that the mafia don was led out of a tiny side gate, to get to which he walked past Cell 16. From there, he climbed a ladder that was placed just for him. He climbed up the stairs and onto the other side of the wall to freedom, where allegedly two cars were waiting to drive him away.[12]

There was another theory that said that there could be a high chance of Bakhia escaping from the country in an Arab dhow.[13]

Investigations into how Bakhia flew the coop revealed that he had found a willing ally in Kamat, a man he had known for years. Kamat was the assistant motor vehicle inspector in the department in Daman, and an old associate of Bakhia. He was known as a man who advanced his career by usurping authority and was seemingly very comfortable with being corrupt. This was a known fact! Kamat was transferred to Goa after the

---

[12]Ibid.

[13]'Bakhia Could Have Fled by Sea', *The Times of India* (1861–current), 9 June 1982

government changed in 1980. He was posted here previously as part of the education department. He, in a power bid, claimed seniority, and he was made in-charge of Fort Aguada Jail.[14]

When his old friend was interned in the same prison as the one he served in, it should have been a foregone conclusion that an escape was imminent.

In the aftermath of Bakhia waltzing out of Fort Aguada Jail, Kamat's and his assistant Fernandes's houses were raided. In these raids, they found gold ornaments worth ₹2 lakh, fixed deposits worth ₹99,000. Kamat refuted these allegations of corruption and claimed that whatever was found were his life's earnings. Despite Kamat's protests, he was arrested for colluding with Bakhia. It became quite obvious that there was no other way that the smuggler could have made it out of prison without some help from an insider. And in this case it was quite apparent that the help came from an old friend. In a spate of arrests, 12 people were put behind bars. Things got a bit murky with the sudden disappearance and death of Sadanand Apa Parab Salcar, the jailer, whose body was found on a beach two days later.

However, a few months later, Bakhia decided to turn himself in, but not after carefully playing his cards. He got his wife, Manekben, who was expecting their child, to file a writ petition to the court of G.F. Cuoto, the judicial commissioner of Goa. The judicial commissioner stayed the detention order and gave Bakhia strict orders to visit the police every Monday till he appeared in court on 31 July 1982. In the interim, the income tax department wrote to the Daman police demanding the arrest

---

[14] M.J. Kamalakar, 'Jailer Held Door Open for Bakhia', *The Times of India* (1861–current), 4 June 1982

of Bakhia on the variety of bailable and non-bailable offences against him, but they did not respond.

He was finally going to be tried for the crossword scheme of 1969.

This was not the last time Bakhia gave the police the slip. A year later, the hearings began and he was caught between the tussle of being pronounced guilty or not guilty. Bakhia, on 16 September 1983, right before his bail was to be rejected by the sessions court, disappeared at around 3.20 p.m. He evaded capture for the next three months, when again the court asked him to appear regularly in front of them.[15]

He was caught again in December 1983 and released shortly after. Then again he was arrested in 1990. All this while denying vehemently that he was a smuggler and saying that he had never seen a bar of gold in his life. The evidence against Bakhia was always scant and he managed to preserve his supposed innocence behind several steps of misdirection.[16]

If he had not seen a bar of gold ever is up for moot, but according to reports, his word had a greater purchasing power than gold. He had lost an obscene amount of money in a transaction gone wrong, which had left his organization's future uncertain in the early '70s. However, he borrowed money in his name, restarted it and repaid every penny![17]

---

[15] P.K. Surendran, 'Bakhia Continues to Play Hide-and-Seek', *The Times of India* (1861–current), 3 October 1983

[16] Justice A. Qureshi, Sukar Naran Bakhia vs R.P. Shah And Anr. on 25 April 1984

[17] Asoka Raina, 'The Don of Daman', *India Today*, 15 May 1982, https://www.indiatoday.in/magazine/crime/story/19820515-underworld-don-sukur-naran-bakhia-finally-arrested-by-custom-officials-in-daman-771799-2013-10-16, last accessed on 29 January 2020

After all, one invests in institutions and Bakhia had the manpower to prove it—he controlled the movement of goods from Daman to Bombay.

After running from the police, he gave up the world of crime and entered real estate, eventually dying in 1996.

five

Mir Laik Ali:
Getting Our Man Out

> Mir Laik Ali, former Prime Minister of Hyderabad who was under house arrest along with other ministers of his Cabinet after the 'police action' against the State, escaped from custody together with the members of his family consisting his wife, five daughters and his only son aged nine. The news of his escape spread like wildfire and caused great sensation in the State.[1]

On the morning of 7 March 1950, shortly after the newly declared Republic of India celebrated its first Holi, the front page of every newspaper in the country announced this security lapse in bold letters. In the process, the Government of India, which was not even two months old, faced its first public mishap. And from a man who, not months ago, had threatened the very

---

[1] 'Laik Ali Escapes from Custody: Vigorous Country-Wide Search Ordered', *The Times of India* (1861–current), 7 March 1950; ProQuest Historical Newspapers: *The Times of India*, pg. 1

geographical integrity of the Union of India.

A nationwide search was immediately called upon; police officers from Hyderabad to Punjab were on the lookout for the last prime minister (PM) of the Hyderabad State.

Laik Ali was a small man, with a wheatish complexion and white hair.[2] And now, his description was of the utmost importance, as rumours about his escape spread like wildfire. The one doing the rounds, from street corners to the Parliament, was that Laik Ali had changed his appearance by growing his hair and beard. Durgābāi Deshmukh, a freedom fighter and parliamentarian, as well as other MPs, asked for a clarification during the Question Hour as to whether or not Laik Ali had changed his guise!

Two days later, on 9 March, India's deputy PM, Sardar Vallabhbhai Patel, stood in the well of the Parliament and tried to answer the volley of questions that MPs shot at him. The question whose answer they were looking for, along with the rest of the nation, was: How did one of India's most influential political prisoners escape from under the nose of the sentries that were guarding his house? A recurring question and rumour about the change in his appearance had to be put to rest immediately. 'It is wrong to assume that he [Mir Laik Ali] has grown a beard,' said a solemn deputy PM. 'The reports that say he has grown a beard are unfounded.'[3]

---

[2] A report on his appearance was sent to all major newspapers and publications.

[3] 'No discussion on Mir Laik Ali's Escape: Adjournment Motion in

The police promptly rounded up all the remaining members of Laik Ali's Cabinet and sent them to the Central Jail in Hyderabad to keep them from fleeing. And then began a nationwide manhunt for a person who wanted to keep Hyderabad independent.

Mir Laik Ali had, in the aftermath of Independence and Partition, stood his ground, along with the Nizam of Hyderabad and Kasim Razvi, the head of the most important political party in the State—Majlis-e-Ittehadul Muslimeen (MIM)—for an independent Hyderabad.

On 15 August 1947, when India attained independence, the slow process of consolidating, unifying and realizing the idea of India that had captured the imagination of millions during the freedom struggle began with a fierce determination. One by one, many smaller principalities promptly acceded to the Union of India or Pakistan. However, one refused to comply.

As an article aptly titled 'Hyderabad: The Holdout' published in *Time* magazine eloquently said, 'Since India and Pakistan became independent just one year ago, 561 of 562 Princely States have joined either one dominion or the other: The holdout is Hyderabad.'[4] As outlined in Nisid Hajari's seminal book, *Midnight's Furies: The Deadly Legacy of India's Partition*, the Princely State became the last ground for battle between Muhammad Ali Jinnah and Pandit Jawaharlal Nehru. The Nizam began playing Jinnah and Nehru against each other in the hope that in the middle he would be able to eke out independence

---

Parliament Disallowed', *The Times of India* (1861–current), 22 March 1950; ProQuest Historical Newspapers: *The Times of India*, pg. 9

[4]'Hyderabad: The Holdout', *Time*, 30 August 1948, http://content.time.com/time/magazine/article/0,9171,799076,00.html. last accessed on 6 November 2019

for his State. In 1947, after Jammu and Kashmir, Hyderabad was the second-largest Princely State. It was bounded by Berar and the central provinces in the north, stretching from Aurangabad in Maharashtra and modern-day Tamil Nadu in the east. While large parts were ceded to the British, the population of a unified Hyderabad was around 16.34 million. The majority of the population of the State was Hindu (85 per cent), which was ruled over by a Muslim minority (13 per cent).[5] The ruling elite refused to join India or Pakistan, intending to maintain status quo and this created problems.

Several meetings were held among the Nizam, Razvi (the head of the MIM) and the leaders of the Union of India, which often led to nought. In the interim, members of the Hyderabad Congress were rounded up and put in jail, and bitterness grew between the two governments.

THE PRESIDENTIAL YEARS

On 29 November 1947, Mir Laik Ali was appointed as the PM and 'The Standstill Agreement' was signed between the two governments. The agreement gave the Princely State one year to negotiate its relationship with India, while maintaining its autonomous status.[6] This agreement did not last its term, and on 12 September 1948, the Indian army initiated Operation Polo, and thus began the annexation of the State.

Ali, an engineer by profession and one of the most successful

---

[5]Wilfred Cantwell Smith, 'Hyderabad: Muslim Tragedy', *Middle East Journal*, 4, no. 1 (1950): pp. 27–51. www.jstor.org/stable/4322137, last accessed on 6 November 2019

[6]Nisid Hajari, *Midnight's Furies: The Deadly Legacy of India's Partition*, Houghton Mifflin Harcourt (2015)

businessmen in the kingdom, was seen as someone who was close to Jinnah, the premier of Pakistan. Moreover, he was seen as a balanced choice, a compromise between the Nizam and the firebrand Kasim Razvi, whose power was growing with every passing day. Razvi's Razakars—a quasi-military force that was part of the MIM party—along with the Hyderabad State Army headed by Major General Syed Ahmed El Edroos were the defence against any possible military action.

Due to his diverse business interests, Ali was close to all sides, including members of the Hindu business community, and was largely seen as progressive and enlightened.[7]

Hyderabad, under Ali, tried to tread carefully and perform an impossible balancing act between India and Pakistan while angling for its own autonomy, but a tightening of the noose around its neck by the State made things very difficult. The Nizam, his sons and Ali were sitting on a tinderbox; an embargo was put in place and food supplies were cut short. The State's airline, the Deccan Airways, was not allowed to fly through India, and trains too were diverted. This isolation left Hyderabad reeling from food shortage, and medical supplies and other essential items were fast becoming scarce.[8]

The Nizam and Laik Ali put Frederick Sydney Cotton, an Australian-British former air force pilot, in charge of flying in large amounts of medical aid and later weapons to Hyderabad. One consignment after another were flown through Pakistan to Hyderabad by Sydney Cotton and his crew. Over 500 tonnes

---

[7] Mohammed Hyder, *October Coup: A Memoir of the Struggle for Hyderabad*, Roli Books (2012)

[8] Nisid Hajari, *Midnight's Furies: The Deadly Legacy of India's Partition*, Houghton Mifflin Harcourt (2015)

of weapons were bought. Moreover, Hyderabad gave the government of Pakistan a loan of ₹20 lakh, which, if used, would destabilize India's government.

On 11 August 1948, Sardar Patel again stood in the well of the Parliament and spoke on the looming problem for Hyderabad, explaining the contents of a white paper about the future of Hyderabad State.[9] He rallied the government to end the uncertainty of Hyderabad. On 13 September, almost a month later, he sent in the Indian Army and thus began Operation Polo. It was over in five days, and on 17 September, Hyderabad was formally absorbed by the Union of India.

Laik Ali was asked to step down on 16 September, along with his Cabinet, after which the Nizam handed over control to India's envoy, K.M. Munshi. The Cabinet, along with the now ex-PM, was rounded up and put under house arrest where they were to spend the next several years in captivity until the State is fully integrated into the Union of India. Detentions for several leaders and activists went on until 1953.

His 'prison' was his luxurious villa in Hyderabad, where he spent the year reading books, magazines and newspapers. In an interview he gave to the United Press of America, the former PM said that he had not been badly treated nor did he keep ill during his imprisonment. However comfortable the lodgings might have been, there certainly were places he had to be and purposes he had to fulfil.

---

[9] *The Times of India*. Indian Government White Paper on Hyderabad, 10 August 1948

THE ESCAPE

A year and six months had passed since Operation Polo, and Laik Ali and his family were still in Hyderabad, unable to get out. They were living in their house under constant surveillance. They saw no way out or reprieve from house arrest. Laik Ali was an important man and was needed back in Pakistan. At the same time, he wanted to fight further for the autonomy of Hyderabad. So they began devising a plan to get him out of India and enlisted help from friends and family and other resources, including the bureaucracy from Pakistan that would help with extraction.

The timing of the escape was picked carefully. On 4 March 1950, the entire country would be celebrating Holi, the festival of spring. During this time, the number of people coming in and out of the former PM of Hyderabad's house would exponentially increase, with mendicants and other large groups entering the large compound of the villa and asking for money and sweets. This would serve as a perfect cover.[10]

Once the date was decided, it was just a matter of putting the pieces together. The task of facilitating Ali's escape was entrusted to an American engineer by the name of B.C. Meyers. The role of the Americans in helping Pakistan is well-documented. The US was one of the first countries to recognize Pakistan and has continued to offer it assistance for several decades, and over and above that, the Nizam and his court had relied on the help of Sydney Cotton, a former MI6 agent, to bring arms into

---

[10] 'Criminal Conspiracy in Laik Ali Escape, Plan Unfolded in Chargesheet Against Accused', *The Times of India*, 28 April 1950

the State to help arm General El Edroos's army.[11]

On 10 February 1950, a little less than a month before the escape, Meyers landed in the city on a mission: it was his duty to set in motion the plan to extradite Ali from imprisonment. Meeting Ali was very difficult, as eight sentries guarded the house, and it was under constant surveillance. The American engineer made his way to meet Naziruddin Mahmood, Ali's nephew. They met to chalk out the details of the plan to escape and set in motion the various pieces that would be required to extradite Ali.

The wealthy businessman was one of Jinnah's most trusted men and in the wake of the Partition, Ali was constantly required in Pakistan. When he was made the PM of Hyderabad State, he was 'borrowed' for that period of time. And having him held in Hyderabad was out of the question!

Ali had business interests in the State that cut across religions and was seen as an enlightened voice around whom a rather puppet Cabinet was built.[12] Ali was used as a liaison with Pakistan. In the run-up to Operation Polo, he made several clandestine trips to Karachi to meet Jinnah to ask for advice and discuss possibilities of aid. When Jinnah died in September 1948, right after the Indian troops entered the Princely State, firmly establishing control over the territory, it did not reduce Ali's standing in the country.[13] While the sway Hyderabad held abruptly ended with the police action, the former PM had not lost his importance. According to the charge sheet, it seems like a large part of the Pakistani State machinery was mobilized to 'bring him back'.

---

[11] Nisid Hajari, *Midnight's Furies: The Deadly Legacy of India's Partition*, Houghton Mifflin Harcourt (2015)
[12] Mohammed Hyder, *October Coup: A Memoir of the Struggle for Hyderabad*, Roli Books (2012)
[13] Ibid.

Mahmood relayed the information to Ali, and after consultation, gave Meyers a letter that he had to deliver to Moin Nawaz Jung, the ex-finance minister of Hyderabad State, who was in Karachi. Jung was to handle the affair on the Pakistani side, putting together the necessary documents and paperwork for the escape. Meyers left the city three days after he landed. On 13 February, he left Hyderabad and made his way back to Pakistan only to return within a week with two other aides, Zakuddin and Ahmed Ali Khan, who were absolutely essential in organizing and making arrangements for the impending getaway. Zakuddin was central to the escape; his mobility allowed him to ferry letters and information from Hyderabad and Bombay.

In the meantime, Meyers brought a letter addressed to the Permit Officer in Bombay for Ikramullah, an ICS officer and foreign secretary in the government of Pakistan. The letter was handed to Mahmood, who showed it to Ali. Then, the letter was handed to one of the aides who proceeded to leave for Bombay. On reaching Bombay, Zakuddin got in touch with Shaikh Muhammed Ibrahim, a businessman who was close to Ali, who was then left in charge of buying tickets and arranging the permits.[14]

Now it was just a matter of getting Ali out of the house. But before it could be done, a trusted aide was sent to Bombay to find out whether the 'state of affairs' were conducive to safe passage to Pakistan. On 26 February, they returned to Hyderabad and informed Shoukatunnissa, the sister of Ali, that all was in order.

---

[14] 'Criminal Conspiracy in Laik Ali Escape, Plan Unfolded in Chargesheet Against Accused', *The Times of India*, 28 April 1950

With the tickets bought and money arranged—Ali was given ₹25,000 for covering the expense of the escape—the family began to leave the country in stages.

On 2 March, Ali's daughter Laeeka, along with two other men, left Hyderabad for Bombay. The three of them took the train and when they got there, Sheikh Ibrahim, a close aide of the family, harboured them. Earlier that day, Meyers too made his way to Bombay entrusted with a letter.

On 3 March, Saida, the second daughter of Ali, Zakuddin and another man, too, made their way to Bombay via train.

In the meantime, Shaikh Ibrahim had outlined the escape route to Sharfuddin, the driver of the Alis. He was to park the car behind the bungalow near a back room. The importance of this had been impressed upon the driver, who complied almost willingly. The car pulled up at the predetermined spot. Mrs Ali, on seeing the car, began the last bits of preparation, which involved giving all the servants money for Holi.[15]

Ali, aided by his old servant Abdul Aziz, slunk into the car without being seen. He was made to lie flat in the luggage section of the car, which was meant for women and had the purdah around the windows. In Hyderabad, women-only cars were veiled and not checked with the same care as others. Ali kept his head low as he lay down between the back seat and the front, in the place where people put their feet. There were gifts piled high in the car, so when it came to the gate of the house, it being a car meant for women only, the guards gave it just a cursory look.

Sharfuddin passed the checkpost and he said that he was going to get petrol filled in the car and set out with its

---

[15] *The Times of India*, 'Mir Laik Ali Escapes from Custody', 7 March 1950

precious cargo lying flat in the back. The car drove down to Shoukatnnissa's house without stopping. Meanwhile, back at the bungalow, Ali Bin Syed, one of the old and trusted servants of the family, was putting on a show! He was passing out cash to all the other servants and those coming in for Holi like nothing had happened.[16]

At his sister's house, he quickly bade farewell to everyone and was put into a taxi that drove him and another aide to the railway station in Gulbarga. Once there, they boarded the same train Sadia and Zakuddin were on. They reached Dadar, where they were greeted by Shaikh Ibrahim, and driven to the Santa Cruz airport where Meyers, Laeeka, Sadia and Ali boarded a private chartered plane and flew to Karachi. The next day, Mrs Ali, under a false name, boarded a flight to Bombay, where again Shaikh Ibrahim waited with a permit, and she left for Karachi.[17]

What followed the escape was a series of arrests, an investigation and a trial that lasted for months. All of the former Cabinet members were pulled out of the house arrest and put in prison. During the investigation, led by Narendra Sinha, Deputy Superintendent of Police, it was revealed that a total of 26 people were arrested for conspiracy, aiding and abetting the escape of Ali. Shoukatnnissa was immediately arrested and put on trial, which turned out to be a fascinating one itself. The case was centred on the validity of detention or house arrest of Ali. As it had been passed before the Republic of India was formed in January 1950, it should have ceased to have any force in the

---

[16]'Criminal Conspiracy in Laik Ali Escape, Plan Unfolded in Chargesheet Against Accused', *The Times of India*, 28 April 1950
[17]Ibid.

new country. While lawyers argued, one by one the 26 charged escaped the country!

In the intervening weeks, the government stood in shock at having lost such an important political prisoner. There were arrests and rumour after rumour spread through the countryside. The police arrested men who looked like or were suspected to be Ali. However, the real Ali was out of the country and on a clear mission—to present the case of Hyderabad to the United Nations (UN).[18]

As a news report outlines, 'Mir Laik Ali, former PM of Hyderabad, who escaped from house custody, was discovered earlier this week. He has crossed the Indian border according to a message received by a relative here. For reasons of security, his present whereabouts have been kept a secret. Mir Laik Ali is expected to reach Lake Success shortly.'[19]

Many years after the Partition, Ali continued to fight for his beloved Hyderabad. He penned several books on the peculiar case of the State that wanted to be a country but was eventually annexed. He died in 1971 in New York after serving in Pakistan's foreign service.

---

[18]'Mir Laik Ali Escapes to Karachi by Air', *The Times of India*, 16 March 1950
[19]'Laik Ali Crosses Indian Border', *The Times of India* (1861–current), 10 March 1950

six

Nabha:
Gangsters, Terrorists and the Systemic Rot

A week had gone by and there were no additional breakthroughs, no tangible leads and the arrests that had been made were just plain dumb luck. The state police was exactly where it had been, and was moving around in circles. They had only managed to nab one of the escapees and one accomplice while the remaining 10 were still absconding.

All they had was the footage of a Toyota Fortuner speeding away at breakneck speed from the Nabha jail premises with the six assailants and the escapees. Little did the authorities know that thousands of miles away in a little control room in Hong Kong, Ramanjit Singh, aka Romi, was sitting with a phone glued to his ear, coordinating the last leg of the escape—that no one gets caught.[1]

---

[1] ANI, 'Nabha Jail Break Mastermind Ramanjit Singh aka Romi Arrested in Hong Kong', DNA, 24 February 2018, https://www.dnaindia.com/india/report-nabha-jail-break-mastermind-ramanjit-singh-aka-romi-arrested-in-hong-kong-2588014, last accessed on 6 November 2019

The national dailies were baffled at the sheer daring of the escape, unable to reconcile what the motivation of such an act was. Was it criminal? Terror-related? Or was it political? The Opposition was outraged, the Chief of the Punjab unit of the INC 'shouted themselves hoarse' over the alleged conspiracy of using the escaped gang members to sway the course of the upcoming state elections.[2]

However, this is not just a story about a daring escape. It is also a story of the systemic problems that riddled prisons not only in Punjab but elsewhere in India. During times of insurgency, in the '80s and mid-'90s, jails in Punjab served as centres of recruitment. Nearly a decade on, seasoned and hardened criminals continue managing their networks from inside. The networking possibilities of prisons are immense. Prisons in Punjab hold a diverse set of criminals, from former ultras and leaders of several pro-Khalistan groups to drug peddlers and international kingpins. Combined with poorly trained armed personnel, crumbling and overstressed infrastructure and a top brass of officials unwilling to act upon reports and alerts, the jail is waiting to be gamed. All escapes utilize similar kinks and move in circles. Whatever happened on 27 November 2016, in Patiala's Nabha Jail, was another escape waiting to happen.

THE ESCAPE

Around 8.30 in the morning of 27 November, a Sunday, two cars, both white but of different make—a Toyota Fortuner and

---

[2] Amit Agnihotri, 'Nabha Jailbreak: Was the ISI involved?' Rediff.com, 12 December 2016, https://www.rediff.com/news/report/nabha-jailbreak-was-the-isi-involved/20161212.htm, last accessed on 6 November 2019

a Hyundai Verna—drove up to the gates of Nabha Central Jail, one of the most secure prisons in Punjab. A heavily fortified building, with radial barracks on the inside, it has two gates: a main gate and an inside secure gate that lies 50 metres apart.[3]

The cars stopped outside and five men dressed as police officers stepped out. On being asked the purpose of their visit, they informed the guards that they had come to drop off a prisoner. They were immediately let in, without the sentries bothering to check their identity cards at the gate. They walked past the gate looking around at the familiar visage; after all, they had been WhatsApped images and videos of the jail.[4] They walked through the dimly lit passage between the two gates, which helped them maintain their cover. At times they would hold the gun strapped to their chest tighter. Those two minutes must have felt like a lifetime.[5]

The guards headed towards the prisoner drop-off point and made their way to the prison warden's office. They went through the routine prisoner drop procedures, quickly pouring

---

[3] Jyoti Kamal, 'Timeline of Nabha Jailbreak and Profile of Escaped Criminals and Terrorists', News 18, 28 November 2016, https://www.news18.com/news/india/timeline-of-nabha-jailbreak-and-profile-of-escaped-criminals-and-terrorists-1316966.html, last accessed on 6 November 2019

[4] ANI, 'Punjab: Nabha Jail Break Mastermind Arrested in Hong Kong', *India Today*, 23 February 2018, https://www.indiatoday.in/india/story/punjab-nabha-jail-break-mastermind-arrested-in-hong-kong-1176448-2018-02-23, last accessed on 6 November 2019

[5] S. Raju, 'Nabha Jailbreak: How Gangster Palwinder Singh Executed the Daring Escape', *Hindustan Times*, 28 November 2016, https://www.hindustantimes.com/punjab/nabha-jailbreak-how-gangster-palwinder-singh-executed-the-daring-escape/story-6sfUmYDn57ee9jPElAvecP.html, last accessed on 6 November 2019

over the transfer documents and the other paperwork. Once the formalities were completed, they were led to the second gate into the main area with the barracks.

Everything was going according to plan. It was 8.40 a.m. The entry process had taken about eight minutes. One can only imagine the guards glancing at each other, looking at their watches waiting to get the transfer done.

Once they made their way inside, they quickly adjusted the weapons on their shoulders, and swinging them around, took firing stance. The guard opened the gate to the barracks, and as he turned around, one of the impersonating police officers, with the help of the faux prisoner, punched and overpowered him. At once, the remaining officers began firing indiscriminately at anything and everything—at the watchtowers and at the guards.[6]

In less than 10 minutes, they were in and out of the prison. They entered quietly and exited behind a hail of bullets; between all of the assailants, over a hundred shots were fired. However, no police officer was hurt. The wardens, guards and the protection battalion were caught by surprise, and they did not fire even one bullet during the jailbreak. In the cover fire, the six assailants found what or rather whom they had come for—the four gangsters and the two terrorists who were waiting for them on the other side. The original plan was only to break out four people, but there, waiting with them, were two Khalistani Ultras too!

---

[6]India Today Web Desk, 'How Nabha Jailbreak Unfolded: They Used Automatic Rifles in Attack That Lasted for 10 Minutes', *India Today*, 27 November 2016, https://www.indiatoday.in/india/story/nabha-jailbreak-automatic-rifles-used-to-attack-354261-2016-11-27, last accessed on 6 November 2019

There is always help for those who ask for it and need it, especially in prisons.

According to the FIR filed at the police station in the aftermath of the escape, the prisoners had ample help from not only fellow convicts, but also two reserve battalion officers and senior warders. Even the Khalistan Liberation Force (KLF) terrorist, Harmeet Singh Mintoo, after he was caught again, said that two jail officers had helped him get to the right place at the right time.[7]

The group did not have any problems in turning around and heading back towards their cars. By 8.45 a.m., they had snatched a self-loading rifle from a guard and were heading backward through the pathway connecting the barracks to their car.

Under the deafening sound of the gunfire and the chaos that ensued, the 10 ran to their cars parked outside and drove off towards the railway line. However, they found their path to freedom blocked by an oncoming train and quickly made a U-turn and headed towards the jail again, firing blindly at the jail. This was caught on a blurry CCTV footage from a shop across the jail, as the high-security jail had no high-quality cameras.

This was the first time that the police retaliated and used a Light Machine Gun (LMG) with a capacity of 10 rounds, but stopped abruptly after firing just 11 bullets.[8]

The car sped away from Patiala and crossed the border into

---

[7] Express News Service, 'Nabha Jailbreak: FIR Points at "Connivance" of Jail Officials', 29 November 2016, https://indianexpress.com/article/india/india-news-india/nabha-jailbreak-fir-points-at-connivance-of-jail-officials-4400637/, last accessed on 6 November 2019

[8] Aman Sood, 'KLF Chief, 5 Others Freed', *Tribune News Service*, 27 November 2016, https://www.tribuneindia.com/news/punjab/nabha-jailbreak-klf-chief-5-others-freed/329051.html, last accessed on 6 November 2019

Haryana, to a town called Kaithal. Here, they parted ways. One of the accomplices, Parminder Singh (Penda), headed towards Shamli in the Fortuner and Mintoo towards New Delhi. Within the first 24 hours, these two were caught, while everyone else was on the run.

SEEDS OF A PLAN

Ramanjit Singh (Romi) had a knack for handling, swindling and moving money. Even now, sitting in a prison in Hong Kong, he is wanted back in India for the amounts he had moved to keep organizations, such as the KLF, that people thought moribund, alive. His Red Corner Notice on the Interpol website has enough charges to keep him in prison for a very long time. However, in Hong Kong, he has spent more time in prison because of the extradition case on him. Of the several charges on Romi, he is accused of funding terror organizations, gangs and the Khalistan referendum of 2020.[9]

In June 2016, he was picked up for a credit-card fraud, but once inside, a lot of people realized his talent for handling money and that too, large amounts of it. That made him extremely popular and an important person to befriend. He spent time with the most notorious criminals and got close to four men who were in the gaol with him. Harjinder Singh Bhullar, aka Vicky Gounder, a former discus champion, whose nickname was Gounder because he spent a large amount of time in the

---

[9]Manish Sirhindi, 'HK theft: Nabha Jailbreak Plotter Romi Acquitted', *The Times of India*, 31 August 2018, http://timesofindia.indiatimes.com/articleshow/65616108.cms?utm_source=contentofinterest&utm_medium=text&utm_campaign=cppst, last accessed on 6 November 2019

playground as a child. Gurpreet Singh Sekhon (or Sonu Mudki), a 29-year-old habitual criminal, only wanted to be a steward in an airline. There was Kulprit Singh (or Neeta Deol), who was wanted in the same case as Gounder, and Deol was arrested at Amritsar Airport. Lastly, there was Amandeep Dhotian, a habitual kidnapper and one of the most wanted people in Punjab, with a ₹5 lakh prize on his head.[10]

This motley crew could have met either in the opening credits of a gangster movie or in a jail in Punjab. They began putting together a plan. The jail was a place they could get out of with the right resources and the right planning. They made full use of the fluid rules and laws of the Central Jail and put together a plan. They recorded videos of the prison on their cell phones for reference. They used their network both inside and outside the prison, activating their contacts on the outside and took extensive help from the friends that they had made on the inside. Later, some even took refuge together.

Harmeet Singh Mintoo and Kashmir Singh Galwadi, two prominent Khalistani ultras, happened to be in the right place at the right time. Mintoo was the head of KLF. And it is alleged that Romi was in touch with these organizations in the US, Canada, Germany and Pakistan, and getting them out was also the part of the plan.

Romi was let out on bail from Nabha Central Jail in July 2016, after which he immediately got his passport, jumped bail and went to Hong Kong. Once in the city, where he became a permanent resident, he began, much like Lau, the man who

---

[10]Monika Malik, 'Nabha Jailbreak: Who Were They?' *The Pioneer*, 28 November 2016

handled the money for the mafia in Batman's Gotham,[11] setting up base there. He began putting the plan into play. By September, he began sending money into the system; by November, he sent about ₹7.8 lakh, and after the escape another ₹1.4 lakh to keep them in hiding.[12]

However, this was not the only level of detail the escapees had access to. Outside the prison, they were organizing their close associates and filling them in on the plan—telling them exactly how things would pan out, the route they would take and the time when this would happen. They even had information on the police officers—how they would react, and the procedures and routes they would follow in the aftermath.[13]

Vicky Gounder had two contacts. One was his close associate, Prem Lahoriya—one of the men who came dressed as a policeman on the day of the escape. The other was Lahoriya's family friend Manjinder Singh, a dismissed constable with the Punjab police. Singh was allegedly the one who had come up with the idea of using police uniforms, the exchange of the prisoner, preparation and vetting the authenticity of the paperwork, and finally guiding them through the various probabilities of the chase.[14]

---

[11]Reference made to Christopher Nolan's *Dark Knight* (2008)

[12]Manish Sirhindi, 'Nabha Jailbreak: Ramanjit Singh Romi sent gangsters ₹9.2 lakh from Hong Kong', *The Times of India*, 4 July 2019, http://timesofindia.indiatimes.com/articleshow/70064980.cms?utm_source=contentofinterest&utm_medium=text&utm_campaign=cppst, last accessed on 29 January 2020

[13]S. Raju, 'Nabha Jailbreak: How Gangster Palwinder Singh Executed the Daring Escape', *Hindustan Times*, 28 November 2016

[14]Navrajdeep Singh, 'Nabha Jailbreak: Year On, Dismissed Constable Who Provided Logistics to Accused Held', *Hindustan Times*, 31 December 2017, https://www.hindustantimes.com/punjab/nabha-jail-break-year-

A couple, Geeta and Sunil Arora, not only provided them with the necessary paperwork and fake identities, but also harboured them after they had escaped. While Sunil was on the run, Geeta's house was raided and vital information gathered. Every single gangster was to bring one or two people who would be part of the escape.

The gangsters had done a dress rehearsal of the entire escape in Moga the night before. They had, by now, complete information of the entire layout of the prison.[15] In an interview in 1998, nearly 20 years before the jailbreak, Punjab's police chief, P.C. Dogra, had said that jails were becoming coordinating centres for militancy. Most of the organizations, such as the KLF and the Babbar Khalsa International (BKI), were run and financed from the US, Canada and Germany. At that time, there were 25 top ultras in prison, which meant that there was easy access to them, and they had easy access to money, which made it easier to recruit, curry favours or even keep cell phones in jail.[16]

Nearly 20 years later, not much had changed. All of them helped each other and every one of them played an instrumental role in executing the escape.

---

on-dismissed-constable-who-provided-logistics-to-accused-held/story-6eilu9rofmIVjRSb4jRrVJ.html, last accessed on 6 November 2019

[15] Aman Sood, '4 Mins Is All it Took to Flee Nabha Jail', *The Tribune*, 27 April 2017, https://www.tribuneindia.com/news/punjab/community/4-mins-is-all-it-took-to-flee-nabha-jail/398155.html, last accessed on 6 November 2019

[16] 'Jails Are Becoming Coordinating Centres for Militancy', *The Times of India* (1861–current), 13 July 1998, pg. 11

NO CELL PHONES

On the afternoon of 26 November 2016, from deep inside the walls of Nabha's Central Jail, a high-security prison, manned by Indian Reserve Battalion (IRB) personnel and protected by 'modern' firearms such as LMGs at the main gate, came an update, a Facebook update.

The notorious criminal Gurpreet Singh Sekhon had updated his Facebook page saying, *'Kaam aisa karo ke naam ho jaye.'* (Be known for the work you do.) Sekhon was not a stranger to words such as those. After all, he had been spending time in prison for possibly being an accomplice in a murder during the 2012 Punjab assembly elections and had 13 criminal cases against him in Ferozepur, Faridkot, Moga, Bathinda and Chandigarh.

Cell phones are prohibited inside jails, but everyone has one. In 2001, Jagtar Singh Hawara had ordered pizza to the Superintendent's office (more in Chapter 8) and Geeta Parmar delivered cell phone batteries to inmates in Thane Jail (more in Chapter 10).

This problem acquires a new dimension of acuteness in Punjab, where despite recurring patterns of escapes, little is done about the usage of phones and deaths in prison to maintain security with severity. Even after the incidents of 27 November 2016 nothing changed. Till recently, short films and videos were released from Nabha, where an inmate was brutally murdered in 2019. If we are to look at the institutional breakdowns in the security of the prison before the escape, none of this will come as a surprise.

OFFICIAL LAXITY

According to the FIR lodged at the Kotwali police station on 27 November, this particular Sunday was different. All the senior officials and guards had left the jail in the hands of junior or subordinate officers. They had gone to Jagtar Singh's house, a police officer who had died of a heart attack. The jail was ridiculously undermanned and underprepared.[17]

Secondly, there were at least four different tip-offs to the state police and jail authorities that something was brewing. According to an FIR filed via wireless communication on 3 June 2016, a whole five months before the jailbreak had happened, the police had been given vital information that could have prevented it. The FIR clearly stated, 'Harminder Singh Romi and three others may try to free their associates.' Romi was out on bail, and he was often seen in a white Honda City car around the jail with a fake number plate PB 11 AX 9515, along with the younger brother of an associate of Gurpreet Singh Sekhon. The police did not act upon this bit of information.[18]

A year earlier, in 2015, the state of the prison and its security were put under severe scrutiny. From the inspection, a report was submitted to the additional Direction General of Police

---

[17]Express News Service, 'Nabha Jailbreak: FIR Points at "Connivance" of Jail Officials', *The Indian Express*, 29 November 2016, https://indianexpress.com/article/india/india-news-india/nabha-jailbreak-fir-points-at-connivance-of-jail-officials-4400637/, last accessed on 6 November 2019

[18]Manish Sirhind, 'Five Months Before Nabha Jailbreak, Cops Knew It Was Coming', *The Economic Times*, 15 February 2017, https://economictimes.indiatimes.com/news/politics-and-nation/five-months-before-nabha-jailbreak-cops-knew-it-was-coming/articleshow/57161507.cms?from=mdr, last accessed on 6 November 2019

(Security) on 3 August, and was completely disregarded; the top brass did not act upon these red flags.[19]

The report pointed to the structural faults in the interiors of the jail, the lack of manpower and lastly how there was a concerted effort on the part of Khalistanis to escape. Secondly, the report found that 56 personnel manning the jail were ill-equipped and undertrained, and there was an urgent need to replace them with an armed battalion.

Lastly, the story of the escape is linked to the poor training of the police cadre. The wardens and the guards did not verify the prisoner exchanged, and they did not follow the police manual.[20]

The police was left clueless after the escape, and the state government under Parkash Singh Badal and his son Sukhbir Singh Badal went into a huddle. Roads were blocked, but it was only the next day that Harmeet Singh Mintoo was caught after he made a phone call, which helped the police zero in on his location, and Parminder (Penda) was caught at a checkpost in UP's Shamli district.

Vicky Gounder was shot dead in 2018 in an encounter along with Prem Lahoriya, and a couple of months later, Inderjit Singh Sandhu, an NRI, was arrested from Amritsar Airport. He used to handle the gangsters' social media profile. An interrogation of Sandhu pointed to Manit Singh Tiwana, the superintendent.

---

[19] Aman Sood, 'Chinks in Security Led to Nabha Jailbreak', *The Tribune*, 5 December 2016, https://www.tribuneindia.com/news/chandigarh/community/chinks-in-security-led-to-nabha-jailbreak/332987.html, last accessed on 6 November 2019

[20] Satender Chauhan, '9 Lapses That Led to Escape of 2 Terrorists, 4 Gangsters', *India Today*, 28 November 2016, https://www.indiatoday.in/india/story/nabha-jailbreak-lapses-escape-of-terrorists-gangsters-punjab-jailbreak-354441-2016-11-28, last accessed on 6 November 2019

Meanwhile, Gurpreet Singh Sekhon was arrested in Moga.

Goppi Singh was among the other assailants in the Nabha jailbreak, and he was caught by an Inspector General (IG) in Shamli, again. However, when the police from Punjab and the state government asked for him, they found that he was never caught in the first place. After further investigation, it was found that he had been let go after he had bribed the IG with ₹45 lakh!

seven

The LTTE Escape:
Escape or a Cover-Up?

If you can think of a way to escape from prison, you can safely bet that incarcerated militants from the Liberation Tigers of Tamil Eelam (LTTE) have done it. In the years between 1991 and 1995, there were 16 jailbreaks in Tamil Nadu, over 112 prisoners escaped from the camps and jails.[1] They dug tunnels, jumped over walls, escaped in transit or just ran away, leaving successive governments of the day completely red-faced. Every few months, scores of militants would hoodwink the authorities and make a clean getaway from the jail premises.

By August 1995, there were already eight escapes in a year-and-a-half and the one that took place right after Independence Day was possibly the most brazen. The direct outcome of this was the tension between the state government and the Centre, one that implicated both the Dravida Munnetra Kazhagam (DMK) and the All India Anna Dravida Munnetra Kazhagam (AIADMK) to being party to the daring getaways.

---

[1] Jayanthi Natarajan, *Clarification by Minister*, Rajya Sabha

Jayalalithaa was then the chief minister, and her party, the AIADMK, had come to power on the pledge to rid Tamil politics of the LTTE's shadow. However, after the jailbreak, she was caught in a corner as she made her way to New Delhi to be held accountable in the Parliament.[2]

At that time, many informed observers asked one question, which got no answers in return: Were the escapes of the Tamil Tigers a larger effort made to keep the facts in the assassination of Rajiv Gandhi and Eelam People's Revolutionary Liberation Front (EPRLF) leader K. Pathmanabha buried?

THE LTTE

There was a deafening silence on the part of the regional parties in the aftermath of the escape. Allegations abound with connivance on the part of the administration and jail officials in the freeing of several Tamil Tigers,[3] a militant organization from Sri Lanka that was founded on 5 May 1976. Like other Eelam organizations, the Tamil Tigers also demanded a Tamil State or Eelam in Sri Lanka's northeastern region and became very dreaded. Led by Velupillai Prabhakaran, it was one of several other acronyms such as TELO (Tamil Eelam Liberation Organization), EPRLF (Eelam People's Revolutionary Liberation Front) and others, demanding a new state. What differentiated

---

[2] V.R. Mani, 'T.N. Trying to Put Onus on Centre for Escape of LTTE Detenu', The Times of India News Service, *The Times of India* (1861–current), 22 August 1995; ProQuest Historical Newspapers: *The Times of India*, pg. 8

[3] Sabil Francis, 'LTTE and Tamil Nadu: Nexus', *IPCS*, 14 November 2000 retrieved: ipcs.org/focusthemsel.php?articleNo=430, last accessed on 14 November 2019

it from the others was how it perfected suicide bombing and guerrilla warfare, using them to kill and maim thousands of soldiers and police officers.

At the beginning of the 1980s, the people of Tamil Nadu were largely sympathetic to the cause of Eelam and the carving out of a separate state for Tamils in Sri Lanka. The brewing conflict in Sri Lanka sparked a sympathy wave in Tamil Nadu. The struggle of the Tamil in the island country in many ways echoed and has continued to echo the demand of several state-level political parties in the south of India who have demanded creation of a separate Dravida Nadu. However, over a period of time, their attitude towards the methods used by the Tigers changed due to their aggressive terror-like operations, accompanied with the constant influx of refugees and the violence it brought in its wake.

Initially, the Indian government covertly imparted military training to these groups. It set up these training camps in various parts of Tamil Nadu. After a point, the LTTE became the most prominent of them all. A Frankenstein's monster, the secessionist military-cum-terror outfit was responsible for the assassination of Rajiv Gandhi. It is alleged that he gave/was responsible for giving the organization immense funding and training.

Tamil Tigers were critical to stoking public opinion and sympathy for the Eelam cause in the '80s, which helped in forging the political narrative of the state politics. They occupied centrality in the electoral narratives used by political parties to garner votes. Before 1991, the AIADMK and the Congress accused M. Karunanidhi of allowing the militants to run free in this state. Karunanidhi was critical of the Indian Peace Keeping Force (IPKF) that had been sent to Sri Lanka to help the government in the fight against Tamil terror groups. The head of the DMK refused to meet the Indian soldiers in Madras (now Chennai). These not-so-subtle 'positions' held by the then chief minister created an air of complicity between his government and the LTTE. This was also around the time when Pathmanabha, the head of the EPRLF—another Tamil-Sri Lankan organization—was murdered in Madras. A few days apart, Indian fishermen and customs officers were kidnapped and police officers were shot dead by the LTTE.

The assassination of Rajiv Gandhi in 1991 exposed the large presence of sympathizers within the government and the state, and their hand in the assassination of the Congress leader. For instance, the home secretary of Tamil Nadu, R. Nagarajan, was arrested on charges of aiding the LTTE. Moreover, there were rumours that several districts, especially Nagapattinam Quaid-e-Millath along the coast, were in the hands of the terror organization.[4] These bits of information led to the erosion of the popularity of the organization and the DMK. The AIADMK, under Jayalalithaa, kept a one-arm's distance from the LTTE after the assassination.

In the 1991 elections, the entire plank of the AIADMK, Jayalalithaa and the INC was to counter this DMK-LTTE nexus, but as the government changed, much of the pattern continued. Once Jayalalithaa cut her ties with the INC, she became part of the same narrative around the issue of the LTTE. Once again, the escapes began with a new fervour. Key witnesses in the Rajiv Gandhi and the Pathmanabha assassinations began escaping from prison. As the witnesses and culprits vanished, the cases gradually became murkier.

---

[4]'LTTE Role in TN Politics Continues', *The Times of India* (1861–current); 27 December 1993

A COVER-UP?

Charles was a coded witness of the Indian authorities, who was arrested a few days after Rajiv Gandhi's assassination. A mysterious man visited Charles on 9 May 1993, and a week later, he vanished from the Madras Central Jail, where he was being held in a camp.[5] An operative of the intelligence wing of the LTTE was one of the men amidst the crowd on the day of the assassination. He was privy to the plotting and execution of the assassinated. He stood a stone's throw away from the human bomb that exploded. He was arrested shortly after the assassination when he was found to not have the official identification papers. He vanished from Saidapet Sub-jail on 16 May, and his escape left everyone flummoxed. That the special investigation team (SIT) officer guarding him could also have been involved remained a speculation in the absence of evidence. However, there are three publically accepted theories on how he could have escaped. The first involved him shimmying up the jail's chimney, running across the roof and jumping past the walls and into a car waiting outside. The second theory involved him unhinging a tile in the ceiling, jumping out of it and escaping. Lastly, that he just walked out of the prison's main gate, just like that.[6]

He managed to escape despite being held in a jail and guarded by a hundred Tamil Special Police officers. His escape was seen as an effort to muddy the waters of the investigation into Rajiv Gandhi's assassination so as to cover up the facts and hide the names of important people believed to be involved.

---

[5] 'The Vanishing Act', *The Times of India* (1861–current), 30 May 1993, pg. 11
[6] Ibid.

BREAK FREE

On 29 April 1993, three more prisoners escaped as they were being transferred from Madras Central Jail to Pattukkottai for a hearing. Kiruban, a man said to be high up in the hierarchy of the LTTE, Chandran and Ravi managed to give the cops the slip outside a restaurant they had stopped at for refreshments. They stopped for refreshments when a man in a white Ambassador stopped at a distance and began firing at the police officers outside the roadside restaurant. The police came under severe fire and the three men, whom they were escorting, did not waste much time and made themselves scarce. In the process of 'freeing the terrorists', one of the constables was killed and another was severely injured. Six police officers were suspended, but again these actions could not prevent the rumours of a Jayalalithaa-LTTE nexus, a similar allegation that had led to the fall of the previous government.[7]

However, the state government reacted to these allegations immediately. The then revenue minister, S.D. Somasundaram, stated that men from the Intelligence Bureau (IB) had visited the prisoners and made them sign documents which stated that the prisoners escaped because of a deal struck between the LTTE and the Jayalalithaa government.[8] This allegation could never be corroborated.

Chandran was the one who gunned down the police officer in Pattukkottai when Kirupan and the others vanished into thin air. He was also accused of placing a crude bomb at the National

---

[7] '6 Cops Sacked for Tigers' Escape', The Times of India News Service, *The Times of India* (1861–current), 29 May 1993; ProQuest Historical Newspapers

[8] Pushpa Iyengar, '6 TN Cops Held in TADA Detenus Case', The Times of India News Service, *The Times of India* (1861–current), 2 May 1993

Integration Council. He resurfaced at Egmore Station, armed to his teeth, carrying a 9 mm pistol, a grenade, two magazines and 23 rounds strapped to his waist. When he was picked up on 4 January, the press was not allowed to photograph him or even let anywhere near the place where the arrest was made. He was taken to the DGP of office, where, on the pretext of washing his hands, he made his way to the bathroom. He dashed in and jumped out of the closest window. Expecting to find soft mud that he planned to roll over and run, his face smashed against the hard concrete, and he died.[9]

Before his failed leap to freedom, he had confessed and ratted out other LTTE terrorists evading capture. In November 1992, 19 prisoners escaped from a special camp in Vellore during a heavy downpour. The prisoners, on that stormy night, lassoed ropes that they had found and threw them atop the roof. Once they were secure, they climbed up to the roof and bolted to the next building, which was a church, and disappeared into the night. One of the guard towers that was supposed to be manned was curiously left empty that night.[10]

Chandran had told the police exactly where four of the escapees were living. A team was sent to Bombay, where they were arrested from Antop Hill.

TUNNEL VISION

It was August 1995, a day after Independence Day, and the public woke up to the startling fact that 43 prisoners, who were members of the LTTE, had escaped by digging a tunnel from

---

[9]"The Vanishing Act', *The Times of India* (1861–current), 30 May 1993, pg. 11
[10]Ibid.

their barracks to the outer wall of the prison. This became one of the most sensational and strange escapes.

The terrorists who were imprisoned in Madras's Vellore Fort Jail simply vanished. The police alleged that the prisoners had dug a 153-foot-long tunnel, which was 10 feet deep and three feet wide, and went under two walls of the jail and stopped right before the moat. Then, in batches of 12, they fled from the prison.

The media was not allowed to see the tunnel for over a week, which led to major speculation whether the tunnel was actually there or not. To dispel these rumours, the police decided to show them the tunnel. Mahendran, a police officer who made his way through the 'airy' tunnel, claimed that it took him around three minutes to crawl on all fours. The police also presented the implements used for the purpose, which included PVC pipes, iron rods and a silver plate. The tunnel was suspected to be dug over a period of time, which is true, because on one more occasion, two years before this incident took place, the police had found them digging a tunnel but nothing was done about it![11]

On 23 August 1995, a livid Jayanthi Natarajan, a member of the Rajya Sabha, who later was a minister in the United Progressive Alliance (UPA) and three-time sitting MP from Tamil Nadu, stoked an argument in the Rajya Sabha, remarking, 'They wanted the militants to escape, and because of their connivance they were allowed to escape.' What followed was pandemonium in the Upper House as one after another member began to poke holes in the story presented by the state of Tamil Nadu.

She added, 'Secondly, sir, my charge is that the police dug the

---

[11] V.R. Mani, 'Journalists Shown the Escape Tunnel of LTTE', The Times of India News Service, *The Times of India* (1861–current), 20 August 1995

tunnel after the militants escaped.' This was a serious allegation of gross oversight. Natarajan further added:

> It will take more than 30–40 lorry-loads of sands to be removed. The police now say that the militants kept that sand, whatever earth that had been dug up, in two to three locked rooms. What were the police doing not finding these lorry-loads of mud? Is it possible to dig such a big tunnel for so many days without the police having any idea, with implements such as wooden rods, implements like nails and old rusty cooking implements? This is what the police says has been done.[12]

Several questions remained unanswered concerning the police's complicity other than where the mud went and the press not being allowed to see the tunnel. The terrorists in jail had several amenities such as a cooking stove, a television and a stereo system. They were allowed to access remittances from foreign countries.[13] Since there was no regular roll call, the actual number of escapees or those who were imprisoned remains unknown. In the Rajya Sabha, the fracas on the escape of the 43 terrorists reached a steady chorus with interruptions growing stronger. G. Swaminathan, former AIADMK MP, stood up for his state and the chief minister. He drew attention to the growing terrorism and militancy all over the country. However, the problems of Tamil Nadu were intimately linked to the growing number of refugees trickling in from Sri Lanka—a large number of them were unaccounted for and roamed the streets freely. Secondly,

---

[12]Clarification by Minister, Rajya Sabha, 23 August 1995
[13]Nirupama Subramaniam, 'Tamil Nadu Govt Comes Under Fire as 43 Alleged LTTE Militants Escape', *India Today*, 1995

he blamed the Central Government's role in training the LTTE, a monster that was created between the years 1980 and 1987. At every turn, he deflected the responsibility elsewhere, but we have consistently seen that no escapes happen without an insider's hand.

The New York Times[14] reported that the entire system aided in the escape. The deep-rooted ideological network, literature and demand for 'eelam', or a pan-Tamil homeland, led to the connivance of several police officers and politicians.

Whether it was the complicity of the police, a large and mighty political nexus or just poor policing, the escapes exposed the balmy nature of security in India. The '90s were difficult for the country, with violence tearing through Punjab, Kashmir, the Northeast and Tamil Nadu. Prisons had by then become breeding grounds for criminality, gangs and making dangerous friends.

Most of the LTTE escapees found their way back to Sri Lanka, moving freely between the two countries. There were several attempts on the part of the Sri Lankan government and the LTTE to sign an armistice. There were periods of peace that would erupt into a full-scale war. All of this went on till Prabhakaran was killed in 2009, thus, bringing an end to one of the most violent periods in the history of Tamil Nadu and also of the country.

---

[14]John F. Burns, 'The Rebels in Sri Lanka Find Allies in India', *The New York Times*, 24 September 1995, https://www.nytimes.com/1995/09/24/world/the-rebels-in-sri-lanka-find-allies-in-india.html?mtrref=www.google.com&gwh=92AE746FBDBC2F88448603C31452FDA2&gwt=pay, last accessed on 29 January 2020

eight

The Burail Jailbreak:
An Endless Tunnel of Official Oversight

In late 2003, strange noises could be heard in the middle of the night from Barrack no. 7 of the Model Jail in Burail, Chandigarh.[1] As it was a cold wintry night, no one bothered to check. Even if they did, little was done about it.

The high-security prison of Burail held several terror accused, spies and petty criminals. Amongst them were three inmates who wielded a disproportionate amount of power within the jail. They were arrested for the assassination of Beant Singh, the former Punjab chief minister. Since their incarceration in 1996, they had made three bold but unsuccessful attempts to escape. Yet nothing was ever done by the jail authorities.

Like the unusual sounds, there were plenty more evidence, which, if investigated into, could have prevented the jailbreak. The least the jail authorities could have done was to ensure that

---

[1]Ved Mitter Gill vs U.T. Administration, Chandigarh...on 26 March, 2015 Bench: Jagdish Singh Khehar, S.A. Bobde: https://indiankanoon.org/doc/55919788/, last accessed on 6 November 2019

an edition of a monthly magazine on prison escapes did not fall into the wrong hands (in this case, the prisoners). Anyone half-observing the trio would have guessed that they were trying to find a way to get out of prison, and desperately.[2]

Ved Mitter Gill, the Deputy Superintendent of Police (DSP) of Burail Jail in 2004, was the seniormost official in the prison. He joined Burail as a clerk in 1988, and with 16 years of service behind him, his authority and knowledge were considered better than his senior's.[3]

Despite Gill's experience and credentials, it was his oversight that led to the escape of four prisoners—three undertrial terrorists and one murderer—in the intervening night of 21–22 January 2004.

THE ASSASSINATION OF BEANT SINGH

By 1993, under the leadership of K.P.S. Gill, the DGP, the militancy in the state had been broken. Yet, the problem was never really solved, and a demand for an independent Khalistan could be heard from different corners of the world. The severely diminished Right-wing organizations that continued to engage in violence and terrorism believed that the best way to invigorate the movement would be to assassinate Beant Singh, who was perceived as the symbol of restoring peace and democracy in the turbulent state.

The Babbar Khalsa International (BKI) is one such organization that was at the helm of fighting for an independent Khalistan. Ajai Sahni, the executive director at the Delhi-based Institute for Conflict Management, called them 'the most active

---

[2]Ibid.
[3]Ibid.

and committed of the Khalistani groups worldwide'[4]. The BKI has organizational setups in the US, Canada and Europe, and reportedly has links with the Lashkar-e-Taiba (LeT) in Pakistan. Sikhs from all over the world fund the organization.[5]

The conspiracy to kill Beant Singh was hashed out abroad.

It was first assumed on 31 August 1995 that one of the three cars in Singh's cavalcade exploded, killing nearly 15 people at the secretariat complex in Chandigarh. A large volume of RDX was used for the assassination, triggered by a human bomb. It was later revealed that Dilawar Singh, a police officer, had got close to the chief minister's convoy and blown himself up. Immediately after the attack, the BKI claimed responsibility, and it was just a matter of time before they were all caught and charge sheeted. Thirteen people were accused of plotting and executing the assassination. The plans were first made in Lahore, Pakistan and ended with the detonation in Chandigarh.[6]

Over the next few months, there was a spate of arrests. The police made a list of hundreds of suspects, and after a swift four-month-long investigation, all of those involved were arrested. It appeared that three members were instrumental in planning and executing the assassination: Jagtar Singh Hawara, Paramjit

---

[4]'Sikh Terrorists, Weapons Caches Seized After Delhi Cinema Bombings', Public Library of US Diplomacy, https://wikileaks.org/plusd/cables/05NEWDELHI4449_a.html, last accessed on 6 November 2019

[5]PTI New Delhi, 'Massive Fund Raising Campaign in West by Separatist Sikh Organisations', *BusinessLine*, 7 October 2012, https://www.thehindubusinessline.com/news/Massive-fund-raising-campaign-in-West-by-separatist-Sikh-organisations/article20511552.ece, last accessed on 6 February 2020

[6]'Chargesheet in Beant Singh Case confirms "human bomb" Theory', *The Times of India* (1861–current), 1 December 1995; ProQuest Historical Newspapers: *The Times of India*, pg. 7

Singh Bheora and Jagtar Singh Tara, along with six others who were implicated and detained. By June 1996, a variety of cases were slapped on them, including IPC Section 302 (Murder) and Section 120(B) [Conspiracy]. They were sent to prison to wait and fight a long legal battle for their freedom. The trial was supposed to be straightforward, and after examining over 333 witnesses, it was supposed to be over in a matter of six months,[7] but the judicial process in India takes its own time.

LADDOOS, RDX AND A TUNNEL

In July 1998, the trio attempted their first escape. The story of this attempt began with a man named Mac, Muhammad Arshad Cheema, a first secretary in the consular wing of the Pakistan Mission in Kathmandu.[8] Nepal was an important channel through which money and contraband were smuggled into India and that's what Cheema, in 1998, was accused of— handing over 30 kg of RDX to a Punjab militant. Cheema was also instrumental in the infamous hijacking of the Air India flight IC814 from Kathmandu in 1999.

The plan was simple: Hawara, Bheora and Tara would use a deadly mixture of RDX and PETN to blow open a portion of the jail. Unknown to the police then, Satnam Singh, a fellow BKI member, had been frequenting the jail, carrying several goodies for the inmates. One such item was a *mithai ka dabba* (a box of sweets), which contained the RDX and PETN. In no

---

[7]Vinayak Ramesh, 'Beant Singh Murder Case: Three Key Accused Escape from Jail, Role of Prison Staff Suspected', *India Today*, 2 February 2004

[8]Ravi Sharma, 'Playground of Spies', *The Hindu Frontline*, 18, no. 09, 28 April–11 May 2001

time, the trio had over 1.1 kg of explosives, which they were to use in July 1998 to blow their way out of prison, but a series of phone calls gave them away.

Hawara, like many other prisoners, carried a mobile phone while he was in jail from which he used to call people all over the world to manage, monitor and plot their escape. He used to even coordinate BKI activities all over the world. On several occasions, he even called an operative in the US on whom the Central Intelligence Agency (CIA) was keeping tabs. Imagine their surprise when they began intercepting calls from a prison in Chandigarh not once but four times. The information was relayed to the Tihar Jail authorities. Hawara's cell was raided and all his possessions were seized.[9]

However, the most bizarre thing was that the cell phone number that was intercepted by the CIA was the same one used to order pizza from a local fast-food joint to the jail superintendent's office! This exposure of administrative laxity was followed by a severe crackdown on the police and the jail authorities. Many officers were transferred, hauled up or punished, but strangely, it did not change anything with regard to how the three prisoners were treated. Neither were they separated nor were they transferred out of Burail Jail.

THE PLANNING

In December 2000, four years before the escape took place, the police chanced upon a tunnel that they had been digging

---

[9] "Tunnel to Khalistan', *Frontline* 21, no. 04, 14–27 February 2004, https://frontline.thehindu.com/static/html/fl2104/stories/20040227004303100.htm, last accessed on 6 November 2019

since June of the same year. The entire machinery of the jail was used to hush up their attempted escape lest it brought harm to the jail administration. It was evident that these three recalcitrant inmates were in possession of tools, implements and other devices to dig their way out of the prison.

Another tunnel, starting from the gurudwara barrack, was discovered in 2002, but the jail wardens and administration filled up the hole before it could be discovered, according to the case judgement in State vs D.S. Rana and others.

As early as August 2003, the station chief (an officer) of the IB, who monitors the activity of various terror outfits operating in the state of Punjab, was certain that trouble was afoot. She had heard about Hawara and his associates and their efforts to restart the Khalistan movement in India. Information was passed and innumerable letters were written by the IB to the Punjab state government, but it failed to illicit any action from the state police. Senior officials were reluctant to follow through with the tip-offs, believing that the separatist movement was dead. The Punjab police's attitude can be evidenced by a comment made by a senior Punjab police official who told the media, 'It was a little like asking to conduct a murder investigation on a century-old corpse. Everyone had better things to do.'[10]

What was really expected happened. Jagtar Singh Hawara, Paramjit Singh Bheora, Jagtar Singh Tara and one Devi Singh—the three main accused and a lifer, a murder convict—finally escaped from Burail Jail on the intervening night of 21/22 January 2004. They had successfully dug another tunnel from their cell in Barrack no. 7 to a small patch where the jail's vegetables were grown. They scaled the walls from there and

---

[10] Ibid.

vanished into the night. It was difficult for the officials to estimate the time of their escape when they found out about it. The officers in Burail hesitated and delayed the filing of the FIR. The police were left red-faced as it exposed their complicity and corruption. Moreover, it became apparent that the jail guards had been siding with the terrorists.

WITH THE HELP OF FRIENDS

More than any other factor that may have helped them to successfully escape, the most important fact that aided them was that they were never separated by the jail officials despite their previous attempts to escape; the four continued to stay in the same cell. This was startling because by late 2003, the number of attempts made by them to escape totalled three. The other factor was that they lived in Barrack no. 7, where the jail's gurudwara was located. It was closer to the outer wall of the prison and was in an ideal spot to dig a tunnel to freedom. The trio were perceived as keepers of the Sikh faith in jail, and each of them was allowed to carry a kirpan at all times.[11]

For over a year, the trio had been digging a tunnel to freedom. However, it was not just the tunnel that was important, but also conceiving a foolproof plan and connecting all the moving parts within it. And it all began with a little help from their friends.

Hawara wielded immense power inside the prison, from throwing around money to officers echoing their ideological stance. He manipulated as many people as possible and one

---

[11] State vs D.S. Rana and Others, in the Court of Anubhav Sharma, Chief Judicial Magistrate, Chandigarh

could beg to ask the question of complicity on the part of the administration, a charge the courts raised during the proceedings of the case. 'However, these accused intentionally and willfully concealed this fact and hushed up the case by filling up this tunnel themselves.'[12]

At another point, the Court Chief Judicial Magistrate, Chandigarh said,

> Accused D.S. Rana, D.S. Sandhu and Ved Mittar Gill used to help the accused in meeting other inmates of jail, other relatives and friends in the office of Superintendent D.S. Rana, and other jail officials accused hatched a conspiracy with escapee accused Jagtar Singh Hawara, etc., and helped them in digging the tunnel.[13]

Lastly, the court accused them of criminal conspiracy to 'wage war against the State by illegal acts of commission and omission concealing the existence of such designs'.

However, this is only a part of the story. Apart from carrying kirpans, they were also plied with a variety of contrabands: television sets, electrical wiring, emergency lights and cell phones. A continuous supply of turbans played a crucial role in the escape.

The court believed that the plan to escape began with an edition of *Reader's Digest's True Stories of Great Escapes*, a book that outlines 42 death-defying instances of prison escapes. Ved Mitter Gill, the deputy superintendent of Model Jail,

---

[12] Times News Network, 'At Burail Jail the Trio Were Regarded as Alpha Males', *The Times of India* (1861–current), 23 January 2004; ProQuest Historical Newspapers: *The Times of India*, pg. 8

[13] State Vs D. S. Rana and others, in the Court of Anubhav Sharma, Chief Judicial Magistrate, Chandigarh

presented the book to Hawara and others. In the aftermath of the escape, Gill was arrested and tried in court, according to the judgement in Ved Mitter Gill vs U.T. Administration, Chandigarh 2015. He disregarded the entire jail manual and let the three do as they pleased. These allegations were not taken seriously by the court and Gill was acquitted and reinstated.

Barrack 7 was largely unpoliced—a little haven within the jail where prisoners could do whatever they wanted to. One such example was the constant interaction between Abid Mehmood—a Pakistani spy held in Burail—where he reportedly met Hawara freely. It is not a secret that Khalistanis have received tremendous help from Pakistan; even the RDX smuggled in 1998 to Hawara had links to Pakistan.[14] Fellow inmates and guards often overheard Mehmood and Hawara discussing plans to revive the BKI network in India. Mehmood's involvement in the entire escape is at best unclear, but he definitely was an accomplice and could have played a role in mobilizing resources for their escape. On the morning of 21 January 2004, both were spotted by the guards talking to each other. During the trial of D.S. Rana, it was revealed that at 11 a.m., Mehmood wished Hawara best of luck for his mission!

The strange noises emanating from Barrack 7 since October 2003 were possibly due to the use of utensils, dumb-bells, kirpans and other electrical wiring to dig the tunnel. The residents of the barrack disregarded the rules of the jail—their curtains would be drawn and lights left on after blackout, or would suddenly go off. At night, the TV could be heard playing loudly. The police officers were scared to venture too close to the barrack, as the

---

[14]State vs D.S. Rana and Others, in the Court of Anubhav Sharma, Chief Judicial Magistrate, Chandigarh

trio positioned themselves as guardians of the Sikh faith within the prison. Perceived as Puritans, the BKI exercised immense ideological and social control amongst the constables and staff.[15]

Nothing should have deterred the police from doing its job. It was clear that Gill had not complied by the jail's manual of rules and regulations that detailed strict monitoring of communication between prisoners and non-prisoners, checking their clothes and places frequented by prisoners, among other tasks.

An escape requires coordination beyond the walls of the prison. Assisting the BKI were several others, of whom the most significant was a Baljit Kaur, wife of Lakhwinder Singh, who was in the same prison as the trio. She had brought Hawara a cell phone, which aided in planning the escape. He had called her 52 times between 12 and 21 January. The tunnel that they had dug ran through the outer wall of the prison. They had also paid off the gardener to help dispose of the dirt and help in keeping the attention of the guards away from the tunnel. Kaur had also organized cars and an outsider, Narain Singh Chaura, was brought on board to kill the lights in the prison. Chaura had spoken to Hawara 13 times.[16]

Kaur and Chaura would frequent the jail and iron out details for hours without supervision. With the cell phones, the plan

---

[15] TNN, 'At Burail Jail the Trio Were Regarded as Alpha Males', *The Times of India* (1861–current), 23 January 2004; ProQuest Historical Newspapers: *The Times of India*, pg. 8

[16] State vs D.S. Rana and Others, in the Court of Anubhav Sharma, Chief Judicial Magistrate, Chandigarh

slowly came into being: cars were rented and clothes bought, money was arranged and an escape route into anonymity was put into place. Now the only thing remaining was for them to leave prison. The first escape attempt was scheduled for 12 January, but it was aborted for various reasons—successful escapes are wholly contingent on external conditions. The course was corrected and 10 days later, their attempt to escape was successful. Subsequently they began to take short recce trips, found the main powerline of the jail and finalized the few pending details.[17]

The tunnel was long and expertly dug—8 feet deep and 94 metres long, it went under two of the three walls of the prison and opened into the outer field in front of a 12-foot jail wall.[18] On that night, Chaura identified the main source of the jail's electricity in the power sublets outside the jail. He put two metal chains on them, thus temporarily shorting the electricity in the prison. At that moment, the three BKI terrorists and their chief made a run for it. They went into the tunnel, leaving behind their implements and 38 shirts, pants and bags filled with mud that they had hidden in trunks and shelves all over their room. A Maruti and a Ceilo had been waiting for them outside. They drove to Fatehgarh Sahib, where they changed clothes, left the cars behind and vanished into thin air.

---

[17]Ibid.

[18]Vinayak Ramesh, 'Beant Singh Murder Case: Three Key Accused Escape from Jail, Role of Prison Staff Suspected', *India Today*, 2 February 2004, https://www.indiatoday.in/magazine/nation/story/20040202-beant-singh-murder-case-three-key-accused-escape-from-jail-role-of-prison-staff-suspected-790649-2004-02-02, last accessed on 6 November 2019

BUT NOT FOR LONG

In the aftermath of the jailbreak, 18 people were arrested, including Gill, Sandhu, Kaur, Chaura and Mehmood, who, oddly enough, were already in jail. Gill was later acquitted of all charges in 2005.

In 2005, Hawara was caught shortly after two bomb blasts in two different theatres in Delhi. Bheora was arrested on 23 March 2006, by the special cell of the Delhi Police, when he was planning to set up base in the capital. The police traced him after he contacted Harjeet Singh Gill, the then Babbar Khalsa chief in the US. After Hawara's arrest Bheora had taken over the BKI.[19] Jagtar Singh Tara was finally arrested in Thailand in 2015. Meanwhile, Devi Singh, the fourth escapee, became a dairy farmer in Pakistan, according to Tara, who revealed this when he was nabbed. Singh had converted to Sikhism and left the country via Nepal for Pakistan.

Both trials of Gill and Rana kept all the police officers involved for years. Both of them were finally acquitted and reinstated. The Burail Jail case remains one of India's most sensational prison escapes.

---

[19] Shailee Dogra, '2004 Burail Jailbreak: Book on Escapes Didn't Work as Proof', *Hindustan Times*, 12 August 2015, https://www.hindustantimes.com/chandigarh/2004-burail-jailbreak-book-on-escapes-didn-t-work-as-proof/story-mWhKGoET1Vbzm3sIlnrcCK.html, last accessed on 6 November 2019

nine

Sher Singh Rana: Higher Calling?

It was 17 February 2004. Sher Singh Rana was sitting on a barber's chair in Moradabad, UP. The barber slathered a thick lather of shaving cream on his face, and someone in the shop turned on the television behind him. The screen flickered to life, and a reporter, in a matter-of-fact tone on a Hindi news channel, said, 'Sher Singh Rana, the killer of Bandit Queen and MP, Phoolan Devi, has escaped from India's most secure jail.' She then proceeded to interview the commissioner of Delhi, who announced a bounty of ₹50,000 for whoever could provide information on the whereabouts of the escaped convict.[1]

Rana sat in the shop listening to the others talk about the fantastic escape he had pulled off. The other customers were trying to wrap their head around how he might have pulled off this feat. They were convinced that he had been paid a lot of money for killing Bandit Queen, which he spent on his escape.

Once his shave was done, he stepped out of the shop unrecognizable even to himself, bought a pair of spectacles and vanished into the crowd.

---

[1] Sher Singh Rana, *Jail Dairy: Tihar Se Kabul-Kandhar Tak*, HarperHindi, October 2012

In a matter of a month, he sneaked out of India to Bangladesh, from there to Nepal and finally to Afghanistan to fulfil the mission for which he had escaped from Tihar, an act that would turn him into a cult figure for the Rajput community in the country. Unfortunately, the journey to acquire this status began with the crime that landed him in prison.

WAS IT REALLY A CRIME?

Despite what he told journalists, Rana may not have sought vengeance by murdering Phoolan Devi. He reportedly told the police later that he had killed her to get into politics. Perhaps he thought that the gun would be his ticket, just as it had been for Phoolan Devi—a former dacoit who now contested on the symbol of the Samajwadi Party.[2]

On 25 July 2001, three unidentified assailants approached the official bungalow of Phoolan Devi (the two-time sitting MP from Mirzapur) in New Delhi's upscale neighbourhood, Green Park. They opened fire on her and her security guard, Balinder Singh, shooting her over nine times in the head, chest and shoulder.

A phone call was made to reporters 44 hours after the shooting. The person who made the call said that the next day the killer would reveal his identity to the world and the reason behind committing the murder. The police, who had a strong lead on the man, arrested him the moment he showed up at the Dehradun Press Club at 10.30 in the morning. Twenty-five-

---

[2]Phoolan Devi, Marie-Thérèse Cuny and Paul Rambali, *The Bandit Queen of India: An Indian Woman's Amazing Journey from Peasant to International Legend*, Lyons Press, 2003

year-old Pankaj Singh, *urf* Sher Singh Rana, who was a law student at DAV College in Dehradun, a liquor seller in Roorkee and history-sheeter, was handcuffed and escorted towards the police van. On the way, he was surrounded by journalists, who asked him the only obvious question.[3] *But why?*

Phoolan Devi did not know that the world was round; she thought that a literal rope held nations together. What she did know was that she had a score to settle. She sought revenge from Shri Ram Singh, a thakur dacoit who had killed her husband, Vikram Mallah, in cold blood right before her eyes, then kidnapped her, paraded her naked through villages and along with others, raped her. She wanted revenge not only for the excruciating humiliation she faced but also for what the women belonging to her caste faced every day.

Caste dominates UP politics and society, which is deeply hierarchical and exclusionary. Phoolan Devi was a Mallah, a backward caste. Those belonging to this caste were routinely harassed by the forward castes, especially the land-owning thakurs. Till the 1980s, UP and its neighbouring states were faced with a law-and-order crisis, and gangs of dacoits exerted considerable sway over the countryside. Many of these dacoit outfits were caste-based and challenged forward-caste hegemony.

---

[3]Sayantan Chakravarty, 'Phoolan Devi Murder: Police Piece Together Puzzle as Relatives Fight for Inheritance', *India Today*, 13 August 2001, https://www.indiatoday.in/magazine/nation/story/20010813-phoolan-devi-murder-police-piece-together-puzzle-as-relatives-fight-for-inheritance-774011-2001-08-13, last accessed on 6 November 2019

Tragedy and public humiliation shaped Phoolan Devi's persona. Married off at a very young age, Phoolan was thrown into the world of crime when she fell in love with a local dacoit named Vikram Mallah. When Lala Ram Singh and Shri Ram Singh's gang mercilessly killed Vikram, she took over as the leader of the outfit, which adopted a 'Robin Hood-esque' modus operandi that made her one of the most feared and loved dacoits.[4]

On 14 February 1981, she, along with her gang and Baba Mustaqeem, another notorious dacoit, made their way by boat to Behmai, a small village in Kanpur district, in search of Lala Ram Singh and Shri Ram Singh. These men were the gang leaders under whom she and her husband had served before they double-crossed them. Over the next couple of hours, Phoolan's gang raided and ransacked the village. Unable to find the two dacoits, a frustrated Phoolan asked her gang to round up 30 men of the village, of which 22 were thakurs, and walked them to the river. There, she made them stand in line and shot each one of them. This senseless act of violence sent shockwaves through the country. After the mass killing, the police manhunt for Phoolan Devi and other dacoits intensified. Two years later, she, along with her trusted aide and partner, Man Singh, and 13 others, surrendered to the police. She spent the next 10 years in prison. In 1994, she was released from jail. In a matter of two years, she was elected to the Parliament on a ticket from Mulayam Singh Yadav's Samajwadi Party.

In 1999, she was re-elected from her constituency and became a second-time MP. However, the mass murder committed in Behmai in 1981 was seemingly not forgotten.

---

[4]Phoolan Devi, Marie-Thérèse Cuny and Paul Rambali, *The Bandit Queen of India*, Lyons Press, 2003

Sher Singh Rana claimed that his motivation was revenge. He wanted to kill the woman who shot dead those belonging to his caste—a crime that his community could not forgive or forget.[5] Meanwhile, the nature of the investigation threw up a variety of curve balls, unanswered questions and alluded to a conspiracy that went straight up, possibly implicating her second husband, Umed Singh, and several leaders in the Samajwadi Party. The veracity of these allegations remains unverified, but what was apparent was that the assassination was meticulously planned in the shadows, and Rana could possibly have been a hired assassin.[6]

There is little or no remorse in *Jail Diary*, Rana's autobiography, and through it, he justifies his actions. Rana rarely speaks for himself and seeks legitimacy, validation and a way to paint himself as a kind, discerning man with the right intentions and moral fortitude. The characters all over the jail—as prison guards and administrative staff in the jail, important prisoners—all say things that feed into the image of Sher Singh Rana the nationalist. He claims to be a patriot, a deshbakht, someone who had done something for his community. He wanted to be respected, and this was a constant insatiable itch that pushed him to escape from jail. The book provides an insight into the mind of Rana and serves as a rich entry point in recreating his life in jail and the subsequent escape.

---

[5] 'Police Have Their Man But Not the Motive', The Times of India News Service, *The Times of India* (1861–current), 28 July 2001: pg. 1.

[6] 'Bandit Queen's Loyalists Allege Larger Conspiracy', The Times of India News Service, *The Times of India* (1861–current), 28 July 2001. Retrieved from https://search.proquest.com/docview/756041984?accountid=142596)

LIFE IN LOCK-UP

While in Tihar, Rana, due to the nature of his crime, was put into a high-security ward. A cell in the ward called the Chakki was allotted to him. Keeping in mind his security, he had the entire cell to himself. On his first visit to the court after his incarceration, he met several other accused, including his brother and a friend, Shekhar, who was also lodged in Tihar and had requested Rana to find a way of sharing his cell. Somehow, the assassin made that happen through gradually convincing pliant police officers who were willing to indulge him because they recognized the 'national service' he had fulfilled.

He has painted an image of Tihar as a society of its own, which it really must be—with its own economy, relationships and rule of law. Rana has portrayed himself as an amicable, upstanding nationalist, who always does the right thing.

There are several anecdotes that Rana pens in his *Jail Diary*. In one instance, he has mentioned how, after the 2001 Indian Parliament terror attack, one of the prime accused, Shaukat Hussain Guru, was made to bunk with him, and he was given explicit orders by the police to beat the stuffing out of the terror accused, but Rana allegedly refused. In another incident, the same police officer who had helped move Shekhar to his cell allegedly approached Rana to make a call to Amar Singh, one of the Samajwadi Party's senior leaders, and a name that was linked to the assassination of Phoolan Devi. The police officer, in the words of Rana, told him that he should call the leader and threaten him about revealing Singh's involvement in the murder of Phoolan Devi if he did not pay an obnoxious amount of money[7]. The 'principled assassin' refused flat out and held his ground.

According to his own 'hagiographical' novel, he made many friends in prison. He grew close to people like Tariq Bambiya of Dawood Ibrahim's D-Company and Sanjay Khanna of the Babloo Srivastava gang. Babloo Srivastava was known as the kidnapping kingpin of the underworld who operated in Ghazipur district, UP. They would eat together, spend time together and Rana's first scheme to escape was vetted by them.

VIOLENCE AND STRANGE MOTIVATORS: A TOMB OF THE LAST HINDU KING

Rana constantly struggled with himself. In his book, he muses several times that he was meant for greater things in life. He had admitted to police officials that he wanted to become an MP and killing Phoolan was the first step towards winning a seat from a Rajput-dominated area. He wanted to gain the sympathy of the community that had suffered from the Behmai massacre. Since he was stuck in prison, he could not garner the respect or the recognition he wanted. His only wish was to become a folk hero[8] by doing something commendable and noteworthy,[9] like his life was consumed by a larger purpose; something he constantly rationalized as samaj seva, or service to the community.

There was a public meeting where Amar Singh,

---

[7] *Jail Dairy*, Chapter 24, Tihar Jail, Location 4731, Kindle Edition
[8] Rahul Chhabra, 'Phoolan's Killer Had Political Stars in His Eyes', *Sunday Times*, *The Times of India*, 29 July 2001
[9] Bhaskar Roy, 'Daredevil Escape Will Make Rana Folk Hero', *The Times of India*, 18 February 2004

Chandra Shekhar, the former PM, and other dignitaries met to demand the Taliban in Afghanistan to return the tomb of the last Hindu king of Delhi, Prithviraj Chauhan. This was a meeting held in Neemrana, in 2000.[10] Rana read this one-year-old report in his cell in Tihar and was excited that this could yield something, and the remains of Prithviraj could be brought back to India.

Sher Singh Rana had found his purpose. He was going to escape from Tihar, leave the country, travel to Afghanistan and bring back the remains of the king. He became restless and began planning.

There may have been another reason for Rana wanting to escape. As his case progressed, he realized that the term he would have to serve for the assassination of an MP, who was also a well-known figure, would be a long sentence, and the death penalty had not been ruled out yet.[11]

HATCHING THE PLAN

In the first few months of incarceration, according to Rana's memoir, he had been given valuable advice by Manu Sharma, the killer of Jessica Lal—a young 34-year-old model—whom he had shot in the head for refusing to serve him liquor at a restaurant in south Delhi.

---

[10] S. Kalidas and Rohit Parihar, 'Neemrana Fort: Heritage Hotel Gets Caught in a Storm as Politicians Try to Gain Mileage', *India Today*, 30 October 2000, https://www.indiatoday.in/magazine/heritage/story/20001030-neemrana-fort-heritage-hotel-gets-caught-in-a-storm-as-politicians-try-to-gain-mileage-778330-2000-10-30, last accessed on 6 November 2019

[11] PTI, 'Tihar Jailbreak: Fake Cop Held', Rediff.com, 29 February 2004, https://www.rediff.com/news/2004/feb/29phoo.htm, last accessed on 6 November 2019

Sharma's advice was useful. He told Rana that it is always prudent to have cases running in parallel outside the jurisdiction of Delhi because it would not only give some respite from jail but also allow his family to save on the cost of visiting him in jail. Rana had several cases against him in Roorkee, his hometown; so, he would have to be presented there from time to time. During his travels to Roorkee, he would always be accompanied by a few guards and constables.

Early in 2003, Rana had tried to come up with a plan to escape, but seemingly someone had ratted on him. His plan was to bribe or overcome his escort on the way to his hearing in Roorkee. He admits in *Jail Dairy* that he had shared the plan with Sanjay and Tariq. On the day he was supposed to leave, he told them that that would be the last time they saw him.

His plan to escape was foiled.

Instead of the regular train and about seven to eight constables escorting him to Roorkee, he was sent by road in a police van. Some 13 constables and police officers escorted him. He was certain that someone had squealed on him, and he was convinced that the two gang members had let the information slip.

A fuming Rana returned to Tihar and promised to let only trustworthy people know about his next plan. He started working on his second attempt.

This time, he thought that it just could not be a singular effort on his part, but he had to rope in more people, who would help him escape from prison. He went to Roorkee for a hearing and met his brother Vikram, who was given the task of finding two to three trustworthy people. His brother brought Sunil and Sandeep—two unemployed boys from his town—who were apparently offered a large amount of money on completing the task. Rana further writes in *Jail Diary* that his biggest apprehension was that these two young men would not be brave enough to break him out of jail, and he would have to provide them the required training.

He also asked his brother to arrange for some money and suggested that he should take it from their mother on the pretext of paying for the lawyer. She gave him ₹75,000.

Sandeep and Sunil visited Tihar four times. In the jail, high-security prisoners are allowed to meet visitors twice a week. During one of their meetings, he divulged his plans, telling them exactly what had to be done. Rana noticed the colour drain from their faces. They were not prepared for something that risky.

He asked the two of them to bring him his brother's messages. He then pushed them to meet him in jail disguised as other people to overcome their fear. He asked Sandeep to shadow a lawyer, adopt the mannerism and wear the costume every time he visited Rana, which was a total of four times. Thus, Sandeep came dressed as a barrister under the fake name Pradeep Thakur.[12] After these rehearsals, Rana claimed that Sandeep was not scared anymore and allegedly charged ₹600,000.[13]

When they realized that they were ready, Rana asked his brother Vikram to arrange for their disguises. He made his way to Kanpur, where the uniforms and handcuffs were bought.

---

[12] Raj Shekhar, 'How Phoolan's Killer Rana Just Walked Out of Jail with Fake Cop', *The Times of India*, 9 August 2014, https://timesofindia.indiatimes.com/city/delhi/How-Phoolans-killer-Rana-just-walked-out-of-jail-with-fake-cop/articleshow/39903726.cms, last on accessed 6 November 2019

[13] PTI, 'Tihar Jailbreak: Fake Cop Held', Rediff.com, 29 February 2004, https://www.rediff.com/news/2004/feb/29phoo.htm, last accessed on 6 November 2019

In *Jail Diary*, Rana has mentioned the outline of the plan. Whenever he would be transferred to Roorkee, a group of 14 police officers would escort him. However, only one would enter the deodhi, present themselves to the guards and process the paperwork, which would include the transfer order. For several weeks now, Rana had been distributing money throughout the jail in exchange of information about the kind of documentation required for a prisoner's transfer—from the list of police officers escorting the convict and their ID numbers to the forms that were supposed to be filled before the transfer.

At 6.55 a.m. on 17 February 2004, Sandeep came into the office pretending to be a police officer of the Delhi Armed Police (DAP). He signed in as Arvind Kumar (ID number 4882) and told the officials at the prison that he was part of a 'three-member team'. He had the transfer warrant and ₹40 for Rana's lunch.[14] They had come to take the murderer to Hardiwar for a case registered in the Gang Nahar police station. He produced the command order endorsed by the DCP of the 3rd Battalion and the court warrant. Meanwhile, Rana had woken up at 6.15 a.m. and presented himself at the gate of the deodhi, eagerly awaiting his friend Sandeep to show up.

When Sandeep arrived, he quickly helped him rush through the paperwork, answering most of the questions, and went to the gate. In a matter of 10 minutes, they were out of the jail, rushing to the parked car so that they could drive off as quickly as possible to avoid the real officers of the DAP and make their clean getaway before suspicions were raised. The real officer showed up half an hour later to find that Rana had already escaped!

---

[14]'Phoolan's Killer Does a Houdini', *The Times of India*, 18 February 2004

It is interesting how popular culture had influenced the escape. Fifteen days earlier, a monthly magazine had inspired the Burail Jailbreak (see Chapter 8) and now Amitabh Bachchan's film *Akayla* had allegedly inspired Rana. In the film, Bachchan's character, Inspector Vijay, arrests Jojo Braganza, a mastermind criminal, played by Keith Stevenson. Jojo escapes from prison exactly like Rana did! A group of goons, pretending to be police officers, enter the prison and help him escape![15] In the film, Jojo then avenges his arrest by killing Inspector Vijay's friends and family.

However, Rana went to Afghanistan for something he had set out to do. Several months after his escape, a video shot in night mode emerged with Sher Singh Rana in Afghanistan at the great Rajput king Prithviraj Chauhan's grave to collect his mortal remains and brought them back to India. Whether he actually brought back his asthiya, or ashes, is unverified.

In 2006, two years after he had escaped, Rana was carrying a reward of ₹50,000. He had come to India to extend his Bangladesh visa and was staying at Hotel Blue Moon, under the name Joy Tirkay. Rana was also interested in investing in business in Dhanbad, Jharkhand, and had made several visits and phones calls. On the evening of 24 April, he had just made a phone call from a PCO near Metro Gali in Kolkata and amidst lightning flashes, he was apprehended.

The operation was led by Delhi's cop Neeraj Kumar, who had painstakingly worked to nab him and crafted the plan over six months.[16]

---

[15]'Nikhil Kazmi, Arvind and the Akayla Angle', *The Times of India*, 18 February 2004

[16]Staff Bureau, 'Catch in Rain Washes Police Shame', *The Telegraph*, 25

Rana was convicted and sentenced to life imprisonment. However, he has been out on bail to marry, or more recently, fight the 2019 Lok Sabha elections!

What is common between the two escapes from the same jail almost 20 years apart is one man. V.D. Pushkarna was the deputy superintendent of Tihar Jail when both Sher Singh Rana and Charles Sobhraj escaped. In 1986, when Sobhraj had escaped, Pushkarna was arrested for not preventing prisoners from getting illegal privileges, but he was later acquitted. In 1986, he was the Deputy Superintendent of Jail 3, and in 2004, he was the Deputy Superintendent of Jail 1.

All said and done, some prisoners certainly get lucky with their guards.

April 2006, https://www.telegraphindia.com/india/catch-in-rain-washes-police-shame/cid/807068, last accessed on 6 November 2019

ten

Geeta Parmar: Karate Escape!

The constables were seeing stars during the day. The male constable lay crumpled on the railway platform in excruciating pain, and one of the female constables was picking herself up from the ground. As their heads finally stopped swimming and the stars vanished, they soon realized that the female prisoner whom they were transporting had vanished.[1]

THE HEIST

Geeta Parmar was married young to Prakash, a petty bank robber who was caught and put behind bars. Without his steady income, she had no other option but to enter the world of crime herself. She became a part of a gang led by Kinit Amin, a dacoit and a drug manufacturer-cum-smuggler. Initially she was enlisted in the gang to carry out petty crimes—she would take cell phone batteries to Thane jail in Maharashtra, where people could not charge batteries for the lack of wall sockets.[2]

---

[1] Mateen Hafiz, 'Woman Convict Escapes', *The Times of India*, 4 June 2006
[2] Ibid.

On 24 October 2000, on the eve of Diwali, eight people walked into B.A. Shah and Brothers, a jewellery shop in Ghatkopar (East)—a suburb in Mumbai, and claimed that they were from the Directorate of Revenue Intelligence (DRI). They said that they had recently received reports that gold was being stocked at the shop and were there to investigate that claim. They asked where the strongroom was and said that they would be using it to interrogate everyone in the store. One by one, all the employees were led to the back room, tied, gagged and bound. Kinit Amin, Geeta Parmar and seven other accomplices made off with nearly ₹1 crore worth of jewellery that night.

Inspired by the famous Opera House Jewellery heist that took place at Tribhovandas Bhimji Zaveri (TBZ) in 1987, the only difference between the two crimes was that the police caught Amin, Parmar and the seven others. In 2000, all of the robbers were sentenced to spend several years in prison.

But once inside prison, instead of reforming, Parmar turned out to be a nuisance.

A VIOLENT STREAK

Chhota Shakeel was a dangerous man. He was Dawood Ibrahim's most trusted aide and wanted for the Mumbai blasts of 1993, internationally. He ran operations in Dubai, Africa and liaised with the Ukrainian Mafia, the Odessa. So it is safe to say that one would err on the side of caution with Shakeel, but not Geeta Parmar, who was called the Queen of Byculla Jail.

Shamim Mirzabaug, Shakeel's girlfriend, was arrested in 2002, when the police intercepted emails between the two, detailing the shipment, sale and purchase of armaments in the city.[3] In October 2004, Mirzabaug filed a complaint with the jail authorities and to the designate judge that Geeta Parmar had beaten her severely on her hands and neck and banged her against the wall: 'She [Parmar] is terrorising all the women in the jail by beating them up and extorting money from them.'[4] Moreover, Mirzabaug accused Parmar of trying to create communal divisions in the confines of the jail.

Parmar gradually established a firm grip over the daily functioning of Byculla Jail, to the extent that in December 2004, an inmate accused her, along with two foreign nationals, of capturing three of the four toilets available to use in the jail. 'While 17 undertrials use three toilets, the remaining 150 have to use the fourth,' she said. Parmar also had a violent streak. When this issue was taken for hearing to the State Human Rights Commission in Maharashtra, it was revealed that when one inmate had tried to use the three 'reserved' washrooms, Parmar beat up the woman, leaving a scar on her face.[5]

ESCAPE

It was May 2006, and Geeta had been transferred from three jails now—Arthur Road Jail to Byculla to Nagpur—and was

---

[3] Niel Pate, 'Shakeel's Girlfriend Gets 5-yr Jail Term', *The Times of India*, 5 October 2004, http://timesofindia.indiatimes.com/articleshow/873747.cms?utm_source=contentofinterest&utm_medium=text&utm_campaign=cppst, last accessed on 6 November 2019

[4] Neil Pate, 'Chhota Shakeel's Gal Beaten by Prison Inmate', *The Times of India*, 30 September 2014, https://timesofindia.indiatimes.com/city/mumbai/Chhota-Shakeels-gal-beaten-by-prison-inmate/articleshow/869370.cms, last accessed on 6 November 2019

[5] 'Chhota Shakeel's Girlfriend Beaten by Prison Inmate', Times News Network, *The Times of India* (1861–current), 1 October 2004; ProQuest Historical Newspapers: *The Times of India*, pg. 3

being transferred to her fourth (Thane). In each jail, she had become too much to handle for the administration. Wardens would shudder at the thought of her and the power she wielded.

According to reports, they said that she would set up gangs, incite violence and beat up other inmates. It is said that Parmar could beat up two or three women at one time. Each transfer gave her a better understanding of how things would play out, from the level of security to the routes that she could use if she planned to escape. She had been shuttled around the entirety of Maharashtra in the hope that other prisoners could be saved from her.

Nagpur Jail had had enough of Parmar and she was being transferred to Thane. In mid-May, she, along with three constables, made their way via train. By now, Parmar was familiar with the route, and at Bhusawal insisted that she needed to get down because she was hungry. The unsuspecting police officer agreed that she could get off at the station and go purchase food.

As soon as she got off the train, followed by two guards, Parmar, who was trained in Karate, turned and pushed the female guard down, effectively immobilizing her, and punched the male guard in his face. Before the third guard realized what had happened, the 33-year-old convict disappeared. The officers immediately went and filed a complaint with the Bhusawal railways police and registered a case.[6]

Escaping is not an impulsive decision. It requires careful planning, an exit route and an understanding of your whereabouts. Why did Parmar choose Bhusawal? It is exactly in the middle, between Nagpur and Thane. With a vast area

---

[6]Hafiz Mateen, 'Woman Convict Escapes', *The Times of India*, 4 June 2006

of hinterland, one can escape into the countryside and not be found easily. It was also likely that she had built up an entire network of thieves on both the inside and outside to help her.

Geeta had a son waiting outside for her and her first impulse was to go to him. She stayed out of the clutches of the police for a decade till she was finally caught in 2016. Putting together several reports, one can reconstruct her criminal record after escaping from Bhusawal. It took her no time to reconnect with Kinit Amin, who was arrested in 2015, and by then was manufacturing illegal drugs in Gujarat and supplying them to different parts of the country. Parmar enlisted her entire family and built a narcotics smuggling ring, which would protect itself with CCTV cameras placed at strategic locations around their base of operation. Whenever the threat of a police raid was apparent, the 47-year-old would jump out onto the street and start shouting loudly about being harassed. Meanwhile, on the inside, her operation would be wrapped up by her son, daughter-in-law and others working for her.[7]

In 2016, bad luck and misfortune caught up with her and the entire family was caught and sent packing to prison.

---

[7] Manish K. Pathak, 'Selling Drugs Is This Mumbai Family's Business', *Hindustan Times*, 29 May 2017, https://www.hindustantimes.com/mumbai-news/mumbai-family-of-four-arrested-for-selling-drugs-to-models-students/story-hqMBUjGx51ocXHhmpjkznN.html, last accessed on 6 November 2019

eleven

Bitihotra Mohanty: 'Call Me Raghav Ranjan'

The first time she met Bitihotra Mohanty, alias Bitti Mohanty, was at a restaurant in the posh south Delhi neighbourhood of Greater Kailash on 10 March 2006. Her friends Thorsten, Christopher Krug and Thalia knew Mohanty and introduced him as a 'nice guy'. Born in Odisha, 24-year-old Mohanty hailed from a well-to-do and influential family. Soon after finishing his B.Tech, he moved to Delhi to pursue further studies. The German woman, 26, was pursuing her MBA at an institute in an affluent part of the capital, Gulmohar Park. They all believed that Bitti was a good guy and so did she.[1]

Why wouldn't they? He was always forthcoming with help, and always ready to travel and had even offered to solve a small complication that she had faced with Ashfaque, a man

---

[1] Prakash Bhandari, 'Top Cop's Son Gets 7 Yrs for Raping German', *The Times of India* (1861–current), 2 April 2006; ProQuest Historical Newspapers: *The Times of India*, pg. 8

she had met on her previous trip, who had begun to trouble her. Mohanty's father was a DGP-ranked officer in the Odisha State Police at that time, and these small inconveniences could be easily handled.

Over the next 10 days, they travelled to Mathura for the festival of colour, Holi. After they returned, they met regularly, and soon after decided to go to Alwar. When they reached a hotel, the two argued whether they would stay in the same room. Despite the woman's repeated opposition, Bitti insisted that they stay in the same room. However, it was her decision that prevailed, and they got two rooms.

'I realized that Bitti was getting involved with me,' she said during the cross-examination by the defense council Rajiv Bharagava. '[In Alwar] after dinner, he told me he loved me, and I told him that I wanted him to be a friend only. The ten days together were only normal friendship. He helped me with my research work. I thought he was a good person,' she remembers.[2] Bitti did not quite understand that, and on the night of 20 March 2006, he made his way to her room.

He entered her room on the pretext of using her phone or having a chat, and once inside, he raped her, 'My friends also told me so [he was a good person], till he showed me his true colours. He raped me and the rest is on record,' she said in court.[3]

She decided in the moment to not fight it or raise an alarm. Mohanty was a strong six-foot-tall man, and she was scared that

---

[2] ———, 'Mohanty Was Only a Friend: Victim: Alwar Rape', *The Times of India* (1861–current), 2 April 2006; ProQuest Historical Newspapers: *The Times of India*, pg. 8
[3] Ibid.

he would kill her or if she screamed for help, she would be inviting more trouble. Later that night, she managed to extricate herself from the bed, go to the bathroom and text her friends in Delhi and Berlin.

A case was filed by the embassy immediately and in a matter of a few hours, Bitihotra Mohanty was arrested as he waited for the train at the Alwar station. Seemingly, Bitti believed it to be just a misunderstanding and was waiting at the railway station to head back to New Delhi with her. The trial began and ended in a matter of 20 days. It was hailed as one of the fastest rape trials in the country.[4] Moreover, the woman was not in the room when the verdict was passed.

As the trial proceeded, both parties tried to prove contradictory views. The defence wanted to prove there was precedence for Bitti to receive signals and the act was consensual.[5] From travelling together to a hug in Mathura, the defence tried to build up a story to show that a relationship was brewing between the two, and hence, it was not rape.[6]

In the run-up to the trial, the German student and her friends began to get a series of text messages and calls from the mother, cousins and aunts of the accused begging and pleading for her to drop the case and to come to an agreement. Under the fear

---

[4] Arun George, 'Explained: All the Crucial Facts of the Bitti Mohanty Case', *Firstpost*, 10 March 2013, https://www.firstpost.com/india/explained-all-the-crucial-facts-of-the-bitti-mohanty-case-654149.html, last accessed on 6 November 2019

[5] Prakash Bhandari, 'Top Cop's Son Gets 7 Yrs for Raping German', *The Times of India* (1861–current), 2 April 2006; ProQuest Historical Newspapers: *The Times of India*, pg. 8

[6] *The Times of India* (1861–current), 13 April 2006; ProQuest Historical Newspapers: *The Times of India*, pg. 1

of danger and intimidation, the police gave her protection.[7]

However, on 10 April, after 16 witnesses were questioned and 20 days into the trial, even while the defense still had witnesses remaining to present, the court would not have it. The judge asked both parties to present closing arguments instead of adjournment and once that was done, the case was over.

The verdict set a record as being one of the quickest rape trials in the country and delivered a progressive and momentous verdict for cases related to date rape. Additional district judge R.K. Maheshwari in the fast-track court said that intimacy shown between two people is not an invitation for sex. In short, the verdict pointed that consent is absolute and has to be enunciated carefully.

On 12 April 2006, Mohanty was sentenced to seven years of rigorous imprisonment in Alwar Jail and later transferred to Jaipur Central Jail.

Over the next seven months, the young rapist slipped into depression, which he began voicing in the letters he wrote to his father.

FATHERS KNOW BEST

On 12 September 2006, Bidya Bhushan Mohanty, Bitti's father and the then DGP (Home Guard) in the Odisha police, began pushing the paperwork for a 15-day parole for his only son on the grounds that his wife was seriously ill. Shortly after a petition was submitted to the DGP and IG

---

[7]Manoj Mitta, 'German Rape Victim Given Police Cover', *The Times of India* (1861–current), 28 March 2006; ProQuest Historical Newspapers: *The Times of India*, pg 1

(Prisons) in Rajasthan; another petition was submitted on 9 October. An inquiry was conducted, and on 20 November, parole was granted to Bitti, who was to stay at the house of a Jagdish Prasad Mohanty. He was not to venture out of the state and had to visit a police station close by every alternate day.[8]

Bitti was released on a surety bond of ₹50,000, but as he was confined to Rajasthan, he could not really look after his mother. On 4 December, the parole period came to an end, but the convict was not to be seen at Jaipur Central. He did not show up the next day either, and the day after that or the day after that.

On 6 December, the police, by now aware of the possibility that Bitti might not return willingly, went to the house of Jagdish Mohanty to arrest the prisoner but could not find him anywhere.[9]

The next day, B.B. Mohanty submitted another petition for an extension of the parole period, but it was denied. According to the FIR against B.B. Mohanty, the police were certain that the former DGP knew that his son would never surrender.

On 19 December, B.B. Mohanty sent a series of faxes to the DG (Prisons) in Jaipur claiming that his son was being treated at an unnamed hospital in Odisha for severe depression and mental illness. His father claimed that his son was in regular touch with the Rajasthan police, but what was clear as daylight was that Bitti had violated his parole agreement by travelling to Odisha and living at their house in Cuttack's Cantonment area! 'It is alleged in the FIR that the petitioner was aware of

---

[8]Judge L. Mohapatra, J. Bidya Bhusan Mohanty Vs. State of Orissa and anr. Court Judgment access: legalcrystal.com/528905
[9]Ibid.

the fact that after being released on parole his son would never surrender again to undergo the remaining sentence and with this motive he took his son on parole and as such committed the offences as alleged.'[10]

The father, meanwhile, filed a case of torture against the Rajasthan police with the National Human Rights Commission and the State Human Rights Commission, on the charge that his son was tortured in prison.

Sixty per cent of all prisoners given bail jump it and vanish.[11] Most police officers do not follow-up, and the laws against those who help in the jumping of parole are easily circumvented. Bitti was one of the 60 per cent who disappear from the face of the planet.

ALL HELL BREAKS LOOSE

By the end of December, it was evident that Bitti had disappeared permanently. There were no signs of him anywhere. It was as if he had never existed. The police went berserk—teams were sent down to Cuttack, but to no avail. His friends were followed. All leads, including a Delhi-based friend who was instrumental in organizing the escape, went cold. The police then turned its eye on his father, B.B. Mohanty.

Mohanty's only son was languishing in prison, and he could not just sit idle. His role in organizing and orchestrating the escape now became the focus of the investigation and on 12 January, the Rajasthan government filed a case against the

---

[10]Ibid.

[11]Pradeep Thakur, '"60% Prisoners on Parole Flee": CAG's Random Jail Audit in Punjab Gave Scary Figures', *The Times of India* (1861–current), 13 November 2009; ProQuest Historical Newspapers: *The Times of India*, pg 14

senior IPS officer.[12] Slowly, the police began to piece together how the entire vanishing act could have happened. As a senior police officer, B.B. Mohanty was aware of how the guarantor during a parole jump is not persecuted; all they had to do was furnish the surety. However, considering his rank, the scrutiny that senior Mohanty was put under was far more severe.

He vehemently denied being in touch with his son or visiting him in jail. The fact that the Rajasthan police had issued a show cause notice against him, despite his rank and the lack of hard evidence, was also a startling fact. Although the then DGP B.B. Mohanty claimed that he was not in Rajasthan on the day his son was paroled, the police had evidence to prove that B.B. Mohanty had indeed been present on 20 November. The father was eventually charged for 'aiding a prisoner in lawful custody to escape...and hiding [a] prisoner wanted by the police.'[13]

The events of the next year did not come as a surprise. In 24 August 2007, B.B. Mohanty was also found absconding. He had been suspended by the Odisha police, a non-bailable warrant had been issued in Rajasthan and had become a wanted man. Even the chief minister, Naveen Patnaik, had given the Rajasthan police the assurance that he would be arrested. Five months later, he surrendered and was remanded into custody, and was released shortly after.

Almost a year and a half later, in 2009, B.B. Mohanty was reinstated, and speaking about his son, he said, 'I suspect that he is dead. Otherwise no son could have stayed in hiding when

---

[12]Sandeep Mishra, 'DGP Denies Visiting Jaipur for Son's Parole'; Prakash Bhandari, *The Times of India* (1861–current); 12 January 2007; ProQuest Historical Newspapers: *The Times of India*, pg 11
[13]Ibid.

his father and his family are going through such an agony.'[14]

It had been six years since Bitihotra Mohanty had jumped bail and disappeared. The trail had gone cold, his father was back in the service and the media had moved on.

RAGHAV RANJAN

No one was actively looking for him anymore until a letter was sent to the branch of the State Bank of Travancore (SBT) in Pazhayangadi—a small town located 27 kilometres from Kannur, near the Madayi hills in Kerala.

On 6 March, Geetha V., the bank manager of the SBT in Pazhayangadi and a deputy manager in the Thiruvananthapuram branch received an anonymous letter in Malayalam. It claimed that an employee was faking his identity and was actually a convict on the run. It claimed that Raghav Ranjan, a probation officer in the Pazhayangadi branch, was none other than Bitihotra Mohanty, the convicted rapist and the VVIP who had jumped bail six years ago.[15]

Many who knew him at the bank and town were shocked. They knew the man as a hard-working employee about to finish his sixth months of probation training. How could the conscientious and quiet man from Puttaparthi in Andhra Pradesh be a rapist?

---

[14] Arun George, 'Explained: All the Crucial Facts of the Bitti Mohanty Case', *Firstpost*, 10 March 2013, https://www.firstpost.com/india/explained-all-the-crucial-facts-of-the-bitti-mohanty-case-654149.html, last accessed on 6 November 2019

[15] Anuradha Nagaraj, 'The Rapist Who Nearly Got Away', *Open Magazine*, 11 April 2013, https://openthemagazine.com/features/india/the-rapist-who-nearly-got-away/, last accessed on 6 November 2019

His educational qualifications were enough to create an impression. He had completed his MBA from Chinmaya Mission Institute of Technology (CMIT) in Chala, in 2009–11.[16] He had also taught at schools, colleges and even at CMIT as a guest lecturer, where he played tennis and sang bhajans with the mission.

On 7 March, the general manager sent the letter to the DGP, who took up the case and sent sub-inspector Anil Kumar Matonandy to investigate.[17] Matonandy had never heard of the case before. Before beginning the investigation, he spent time watching videos and familiarizing himself with the case and then prodded Ranjan/Mohanty.

The tall, lanky man who went by Raghav Ranjan simply refused to acknowledge when the police called him by his real name. 'I am not Bitti,' he would repeat. However, the police did not give up and finally got access to his flat in Zareen Mahal. They found a host of documents, a printer and other related items. This piqued Matonandy's curiosity, and he went through all his certificates and followed up with all the universities. What he found was interesting; however, his handwriting did not match. While the roll numbers in the university documents were real, the name was not. They were registered in the name of Bitti Mohanty.

On 8 March, Raghav Ranjan was arrested by the police and put into judicial custody indefinitely. Surendra Kumar Sharma of the Anti-Corruption Bureau from Dausa, Rajasthan, who

---

[16]Special Correspond, 'Bitti Case Now Enters a Crucial Phase', *The Hindu*, 19 March 2013, https://www.thehindu.com/news/national/kerala/bitti-case-now-enters-a-crucial-phase/article4523111.ece, last accessed on 6 November 2019

[17]Ibid.

had first interrogated Bitti in 2006, was brought down to look at Ranjan and at that very moment, he had no doubt that the man he was looking at was the convicted rapist. He looked at him and said, 'How are you, Mohanty?' He was even able to tell the rest of the officers that he (Bitti) had a mole under his left eye![18]

Three days later, on 11 March, Bitti confessed to his identity, but then retracted his statement. Besides, statements made in custody are not seen as legitimate, because they are often made under duress or coercion.

Despite the statement and documents, they could not nail him down. His handwriting did not match, there was no conclusive DNA proof, and while there was resemblance, the documentation was in the name of Raghav Ranjan. A 20-member team was put together to investigate Raghav Ranjan, but there was no conclusive proof that tied the two men together. They began heading back to Puttaparthi in Andhra Pradesh, Odisha and other places he had passed through and realized that there was no Ranjan before 2007. The next step was to take him back to Rajasthan and match his DNA and fingerprints, which came out as positive. Then there was no doubt that the man claiming to be Raghav Ranjan was none other than Bitti Mohanty. Finally, on 17 March, B.B. Mohanty identified his son.

THE LETTER

Several theories abound as to who had written the letter to the management at SBT. One theory was that Bitti had fallen in love

---

[18] Anuradha Nagaraj, 'The Rapist Who Nearly Got Away', *Open Magazine*, 11 April 2013, https://openthemagazine.com/features/india/the-rapist-who-nearly-got-away/, last accessed on 6 November 2019

with a woman who was part of the same batch of probationary officers, and he had confessed to her who he actually was. Bitti wanted out of the relationship for fear of being caught.

The case took a surprising turn when the family of the woman came to know about her wish to marry Ranjan/Bitti. After the 2012 Nirbhaya rape, his face appeared on national television as one of the culprits who had been absconding after committing crimes against women. They identified him and wrote the letter to the management.[19]

MR MOHANTY? NO, CALL ME RAGHAV RANJAN

The police's investigation revealed that there were two men in particular who had helped Bitti settle down. One was in the know, the other became a mentor to Raghav Ranjan, unaware of his identity.

The first was a 78-year-old retired IAS Officer K. Paramhamsa, who lived in the Prasanthi Nilayam (the abode of Sai Baba) for several years. Right after jumping parole, Bitti went into hiding and resurfaced in Puttaparthi, a small 'spiritual town' in Andhra Pradesh, a few months later. Here, Paramhamsa allegedly helped Bitti Mohanty rebuild his life as S. Raghav Ranjan.[20]

---

[19]PTI, 'Did Love Affair Give Away Bitti Mohanty's Real Identity?' Rediff.com, 13 March 2013, https://www.rediff.com/news/report/did-love-affair-give-away-bitti-mohanty-s-real-identity/20130313.htm, last accessed on 6 November 2019

[20]A. Srinivasan Rao, 'Introvert to King Con: Rape Convict Bitti a Sophisticated Criminal Who Cheated the Bank Officials, Locals of Puttaparthi', *India Today*, 16 March 2013, https://www.indiatoday.in/india/south/story/bitti-mohanty-rape-accused-criminal-german-rape-case-kerala-police-bank-officials-puttaparthi-156351-2013-03-16, last accessed on 6 November 2019

Bitti was introduced to S.V. Rama Rao, a former headmaster of Zilla Parishad School, by the VVIP devotee (Paramhamsa). On the recommendation of the retired civil servant, Rama Rao, who was the then principal of Sathya Saibaba's School for Destitute Children, employed Raghav/Bitti as a computer science and math teacher. At some point that year, the young man fell ill, and Rama Rao and his wife nursed him back to health. During the illness, the two bonded, and Rao even arranged for a flat for him, which was close to his house. Little did he know that the house that he would help the young man get would now become the address to which he would tie-in and build his new identity around. Bitti registered his voter ID to the house in Puttaparthi, opened a bank account with the help of Rao and slowly hid his prior life, one photo ID at a time.[21]

It really is not surprising that nothing was verified, but in smaller towns getting a recommendation from a trusted person was enough. After this, it was smooth sailing. Rama Rao pushed Raghav Ranjan to teach at a university when he lost his job in the school. In 2009, Ranjan told Rao that he wanted to pursue his MBA, and the old man pushed him to take the Management Aptitude Test, in which he did very well and sought admission into CMIT. It was on Rao's insistence that Raghav/Bitti applied to SBT too!

During this time, he claimed that Bitti's parents would frequent 'Raghav Ranjan', and he had introduced his father as

---

[21] Special Correspondents, 'A Fugitive's Daring Trail of Subterfuge', *The Hindu*, 10 March 2013, https://www.thehindu.com/todays-paper/tp-national/a-fugitives-daring-trail-of-subterfuge/article4493512.ece, last accessed on 6 November 2019

a primary school teacher and a family friend.[22] All this while, no one knew whom they were helping.

In 2017, Bitti Mohanty was released on bail.

---

[22] Anuradha Nagaraj, 'The Rapist Who Nearly Got Away', *Open Magazine*, 11 April 2013 https://openthemagazine.com/features/india/the-rapist-who-nearly-got-away/, last accessed on 6 November 2019

twelve

Operation Jailbreak

On the morning of 14 November 2005, the residents of the town of Jehanabad in Bihar, who had spent a night in horror, were still scared to step out of their own houses. The events of the previous night still haunted them; the sounds of gunfire and bombs were still fresh. Hundreds of inmates escaped when the gate of the district jail was blown up. The most notorious of the escapees was Ajay Sao, the commander of the People's Red Army. All of this happened when the lights in the town had gone off.

For decades, the residents of Jehanabad were used to two things: long power cuts and reports of deadly massacres by the Ranvir Sena, an illegal quasi-military outfit.[1] Over the years, the Sena

---

[1]Bela Bhatia, 'Jailbreak and the Maoist Movement', *Economic and Political Weekly*, 40, no. 51 (2005). https://www.epw.in/journal/2005/51/commentary/jehanabad-i-jailbreak-and-maoist-movement.html, last

that represented the landowning forward-caste Bhumihars had become infamous for regularly killing Dalit farmers. Now, a recent third force had come into the mix that sought to balance the equation with their armed force—the Maoists.

Over the past few years, the district of Jehanabad had become a hotbed of Maoist activity and also the epicentre of Maoist violence. The police were unprepared to check the growth of the proscribed radical Left-wing organization. On that day, the presence of the police was sparse. With Bihar in the throes of an election, the heavy Central Forces and the state police had already passed through the region that had voted. There were raids by the Maoists on armouries in neighbouring districts. Unknown to the residents of the town, the police feared that a big attack might take place, but were unsure when it would happen.

On the evening of 13 November, a large convoy of police jeeps accompanied by fully armed personnel in khakis entered the town. Anticipating a violent showdown, many stayed indoors, while other residents scampered to safety and shopkeepers shuttered their shops. Within no time, the town wore a deserted look. However, there was something amiss, and the locals did not pay heed. Instead of wearing the standard-issue boots, these 'cops' were wearing chappals.[2]

Suddenly, a voice cackled through a large megaphone, 'We don't want to hurt you. Our problem is with the administration.' With that announcement, the Maoists began their 'operation', for which they had prepared for months, undergoing gruelling training and drills. Operation Jailbreak was underway and it

---

accessed on 6 November 2019
[2]Ibid.

lasted for three hours, into the wee hours of the night.

The next day, news spread through the local and national media. On the night of 13 November, a total of 341 prisoners escaped, of which 250 were Maoists. They went on a rampage in the district.

It was one of the biggest jailbreaks in the country. A police official later told the media, 'We should have killed him three years ago (when he was nabbed).'[3]

The official was talking about Ajay Sao, alias Ajay Kanu, alias Ravi Kanu, the man for whom the entire exercise was undertaken. He was missing from the prison and soon became Bihar's most wanted criminal.

The next day, normalcy was restored at around 11 a.m. when the police sent in reinforcements. The media reported that five men were killed and 20 belonging to the Ranvir Sena kidnapped. Amongst them was the most notorious Bade Sharma,[4] whose blood-spattered body lay in the district jail, riddled with 40 bullets. A senior and dreaded member of the Sena, Sharma was allegedly behind the 1997 Laxmanpur-Bathe massacre, in which 58 Dalits were killed. The Maoists ended the life of luxury and protection Sharma enjoyed in prison.

The Central Reserve Police Force (CRPF) and the local cops stood over the body, looking clueless, as no one had anticipated an escape such as this.

---

[3]Uttam Sengupta, 'Bihar's Most Wanted: Ajay, in 40s, Trigger-happy and Fond of Good Life', *The Telegraph*, 20 November 2005, https://www.telegraphindia.com/india/bihar-s-most-wanted-ajay-in-40s-trigger-happy-and-fond-of-good-life/cid/839335, last accessed on 6 November 2019
[4]Ibid.

A GROWING THREAT

By September 2004, the Maoist influence had steadily grown into a perceivable threat to the country. By this year, 156 districts in the country were affected by Naxal violence, and by February 2005, the number grew to 170.[5] A year later, in 2006, the then PM Manmohan Singh identified Maoism as the 'single biggest internal security threat ever faced by our country'. These districts included northern parts of Bihar, parts of Jharkhand, Chhattisgarh, Maharashtra, Andhra Pradesh, Telangana and Karnataka.[6] The aim of this expansion was to challenge the authority of the Indian State.

Before 2004, the biggest problem that the Maoists faced was factionalism. Each state had its own military group with its own agenda, cadre and idea of implementation of the method to realize its goals. Smaller factions posed the greatest threat to the success of the movement, which, despite having pockets of influence, were considered a nuisance rather than an actual threat to the state. In 2004, the various warring factions came together to form the Communist Party of India (Maoist) (CPI [M]). This quasi-military outfit was a combination of several militant organizations, but most notably, the People's War Group (PWG) merged with the Maoist Communist Centre

---

[5]TT Bureau, 'RED SPREAD - In Karnataka, Core Maoists up from 25 to 600 in Last Six Months, *The Telegraph*, 6 March 2005, https://www.telegraphindia.com/opinion/red-spread-in-karnataka-core-maoists-up-from-25-to-600-in-last-six-months/cid/1022439, last accessed on 6 November 2019

[6]Saumitra Mohan, 'Naxalism: The Enemy Within, Institute of Peace and Conflict Studies', May 2007, https://www.ipcs.org/focusthemsel.php?articleNo=2284

(MCC) and formed an organization of a trained army with over 4,000 soldiers who could operate sophisticated and indigenous weapons.[7]

There was a steady increase in violent attacks the year before Sao's escape from Jehanabad Jail. The Maoists were trying to see how far they could put the administrative on the defensive. On 6 February 2004, a few hundred Naxalites laid siege to the town of Koraput, Odisha, and brought it to a standstill. They attacked 'the district headquarters complex, made an abortive attempt to storm the jail, but successfully raided the district armoury, looting all 500 weapons and several thousand rounds of ammunition'.[8] Likewise, in 2005, in Madhuban, in the East Champaran district of Bihar, a little over 200 Maoists looted the armoury, set fire to the police station, killed five cops and looted two banks.[9]

Maoists were adopting violent means to reassert their organizational power, especially when the political system was massively stretched, heading towards a second election in a year. They were following in letter and spirit the famous dictum of the Chinese revolutionary leader Mao Zedong, who had famously said that power flows from the barrel of a gun. They were mostly driven by ideology and their own belief systems aimed at correcting an imbalance in the economic welfare and social justice in rural society caused due to the failure of the Indian State and its inability to protect the interests of the downtrodden. Thus, they were called the 'red robin hood', who challenged

---

[7] P.V. Ramana, 'Jehanabad Raid: A Higher Stage of Maoists' Militarisation', *The Tribune*, 19 November 2005
[8] Ibid.
[9] Ibid.

the deep-rooted authority of traditional power structures of dominant castes.

Bihar was again heading into an election for the second time in a year. The February elections held in the beginning of 2005 had thrown up a hung assembly with no clear mandate. In a matter of six months, the state was again forced to face another election beginning in October.

Maoists had been a thorn in the conduct of the polls. During this time, there was a spike in violence in this region. The election schedule coincided with the celebrations of the 88th anniversary of the October Revolution in Russia, what is popularly called the Bolshevik Revolution of 1917. The communists, under the leadership of Vladimir Lenin, had overthrown the unjust czarist rule in the country. The Maoists drew inspiration from the Bolsheviks and wanted to replicate the same there, in Bihar.

THE SIEGE

According to media reports, the police were expecting an attack.[10] They were also sure that the attack would happen after the Central Forces deployed during the elections would depart. As it turned out, this was true. The Central Forces had left the district to watch over the assembly elections in northern Bihar in October, leaving Jehanabad susceptible to Maoist violence.

In fact, just two days before the operation, the Maoists' Central Military Commission had organized a raid in Giridih,

---

[10] Abdul Qadir, 'Operation Jailbreak: They Knew It Was Coming', *The Times of India* (1861–current), November 15, 2005; ProQuest Historical Newspapers: *The Times of India*, pg 12

Jharkhand, where they had killed five police officers and ransacked the armoury for 185 weapons and 3,000 bullets. Clearly, the ammunition came handy during the siege.[11]

The whole operation was impeccably planned to the tiniest detail. Manoj Kanu, one of the Maoist soldiers, was caught when he accidentally triggered a bomb, leaving himself grievously injured. In a conversation with *The Times of India*,[12] he revealed that the training for the operation had begun in the jungles of Hazaribagh in Jharkhand months ago. A man named Gautam trained them. The operation was planned to the minutiae—from who was to be kidnapped to who was to be killed in the prison.

A blood-splattered poster on the wall of the jail detailed that the objectives of the brazen operation to free 'communist revolutionaries along with activists and supporters of the peasant movement...and to give mrityudand [capital punishment] to those notorious killer-leaders of feudal-goonda army Ranvir Sena, guilty of various massacres, who were safe in the jail [sic].'[13]

The three-pronged attack began prematurely at 9.05 p.m., when Manoj Kanu's bomb misfired at the police lines.

Like most Indian jails, the district jail was understaffed and overcrowded. The Jehanabad Jail had a capacity of 140, but housed over 650 prisoners. Three armed police constables and five home guards secured it. The police lines that housed the armoury were protected by one-fifth of the plausible strength,

---

[11]Sanjay Kumar Jha, 'Maoists Stage Biggest Jail Breakout in Bihar, State Administration Scurries for Cover', *India Today*, 25 November 2005

[12]Times News Network, 'The Whole System Supports the Corrupt', *The Times of India*, 15 November 2005

[13]Bela Bhatia, 'Jailbreak and the Maoist Movement', *Economic and Political Weekly*, 40, no. 51(17–23 December 2005): 5369–71

a total of 22 guards.[14]

Meanwhile, Ajay Sao, who had planned the entire operation, communicating with leadership outside, sat in his cell, along with the 200 other Maoists spread across the jail, waiting for their comrades and freedom.[15]

FREEING AJAY SAO

The Maoists couldn't make any headway to get close to the armoury, as it was protected by several police officers stationed near it, with better guns and ammunition. But the story of the jail was completely different.

Bombs began to explode all over the town, and one team made its way to the gates of the district jail. As they approached the gates of the jail, it was only a matter of time before they would blow it up. Eyewitness accounts recorded by various newspapers said that the gate offered little or no resistance to the bombs and immediately fell apart.[16] The Maoists ran in and freed Sao, handed him an AK-47, which he gripped with familiarity. Deftly, with a practiced hand, he joined the operation, his finger wrapped around the trigger, shooting wildly.

Officers at the jail said that it was not easy to handle a

---

[14]Ibid.

[15]PTI, 'Maoists Storm Jehanabad Jail', Rediff.com, 14 November 2005, https://www.rediff.com/news/2005/nov/14bihar.htm, last accessed on 6 November 2019

[16]Sanjay Kumar Jha, 'Maoists Stage Biggest Jail Breakout in Bihar, State Administration Scurries for Cover', *India Today*, 28 November 2005 https://www.indiatoday.in/magazine/states/story/20051128-maoists-stage-biggest-jail-breakout-in-bihar-state-administration-scurries-for-cover-786493-2005-11-28, last accessed on 6 November 2019

rifle after three years of being held behind bars, but Sao began firing with expert precision. His first kill was Bade Sharma, who had confessed to his role in 25 murders and had refused to leave the prison when ordered to do so. Sharma was a class enemy—in Marxist parlance a man who opposed the poor—and they wanted to take him prisoner as a political statement, but that did not happen.[17]

After the three hours the operation carried on for, Sao joined the remaining Maoists, and they vanished into the jungles nearby, along with the other prisoners.

Although he was in prison, Sao had resources and the ability to steer things his way outside the jail. Even earlier, there had been attempts to free him from court during one of his trials, but the heavy deployment of the Special Task Force (STF) had prevented it. According to the police, the Maoists were flush with funds and not averse to bribing lawyers or judges to get their men released.

However, the police feared that if their (Maoists) attempts to free their commander from custody failed, eventually their patience would run out and they would act more dramatically. Before his arrest in 2002, Sao had a reward of ₹2.5 lakh on his head. Now, after the Jehanabad Jailbreak, the police was willing to pay anything to get him back.

---

[17]Uttam Sengupta, 'Bihar's Most Wanted: Ajay, In 40s, Trigger-Happy and Fond of Good Life', *The Telegraph*, 20 November 2005, https://www.telegraphindia.com/india/bihar-s-most-wanted-ajay-in-40s-trigger-happy-and-fond-of-good-life/cid/839335, last accessed on 6 November 2019

THE CONFESSION

In August 2002, the police in Patna surveilled a house, in which they thought the 'commander' lived. They broke in and retrieved a photograph of a man they thought to be Ajay Sao, one of the most feared men in Bihar. The man in the photographs seemed to be in his forties, and it was circulated throughout the region.

A few months later, a police informant gave a tip-off. The man in the photograph had been spotted. He was seen waiting in a car while the driver was buying cigarettes as they were entering Patna. Before the car could enter Bihar's capital, it was intercepted by the police; the man was nabbed and sent to an interrogation facility.

For over six hours, the man was subjected to third-degree methods. That's when they realized that he was someone important because he did not break. He kept asking whether the news of his 'abduction' by the police had been made public. Once he learnt that the Maoists had accused the police of kidnapping Ajay Sao, he confessed to his identity.[18]

WHO WAS SAO?

It was the death of his father, who was killed over a land dispute, which drove him into the arms of the Maoists. An arts graduate from Jehanabad College, he joined the PWG in 1980 to ostensibly avenge his father's death. Sao had a fascination for weapons and was an expert at handling them.

The central leadership of the PWG saw in him a committed worker and that led to his meteoric rise within the organization.

---

[18] Ibid.

He became a part of the PWG's central committee and the region's local commander. However, he developed a reputation of someone prone to unleash violence, which gave him the status of being one of the most wanted murderers in the state.

Sao was recognized as a natural leader, and he presented all the qualities of a good one; he didn't trust many people, he was fearless and was extremely arrogant. He stood up and faced any challenge and always delivered when put in a difficult spot. These qualities evoked a sense of awe even amongst the police officers who crossed paths with him.

During his imprisonment, he was quick to mobilize his fellow Maoists and fight for all of them. Sao led an agitation for better facilities inside the penitentiary. So resourceful was he that he had a continuous inflow of money and access to cell phones and even a television inside the jail. The money would be used to pay for fellow inmates' legal fees, cover the cost of weddings, medical treatment or other issues at their homes. His largesse was not limited to providing monetary help alone; he had a control over gastronomic privileges in prison too. He had his own kitchen, where he would get fish, mutton and other items cooked for himself and other inmates.

Sao had spent most of his time in the high-security Beur Central Jail on the outskirts of Patna before being shifted to Jehanabad to facilitate his appearances in court. In both prisons, he was allowed visitors at all times and got whatever he wanted. He had also gained weight!

The prison authorities knew that police officers were prisoners of the Maoists. Being tough on them would mean being threatened by them, and that applied to anybody. A couple of years ago, a Beur Jail superintendent died under 'mysterious' circumstances after refusing to succumb to pressure. 'Normally, it is enough to convey to prison officials that the Maoists know where their children are studying,' acknowledged a police officer grimly.[19]

The money seized from his house and that of his relative's was stored in Patna Jail, which was allegedly eaten by the rats in 2017! His family had considerable wealth and photographs of them in their albums show them visiting Jaipur and Kashmir.

ARRESTED AGAIN

The Jailbreak of 2004 signalled a new type of Maoist terror, one that was organized, trained and dangerous. The state and Central governments were underprepared for such an attack, despite the awareness that it would happen. While living in the jungle, the Maoists could fight for a cause and live through various hardships; their ideological fight kept them more motivated than the police, and their innovative guerrilla tactics kept the police forces on their toes.

However, in no time Sao was arrested again. Two years later, he was caught in Tankuppa,[20] with a gun and six bullets by a joint operation of the STF, Bihar Police and Central Intelligence. Today, he is held in Patna Jail, serving a life sentence along with three of his family members.

---

[19]Ibid.
[20]PTI, '1,500 Kg of Explosives Seized from Gaya Forest', Rediff.com, 10 February 2010, https://www.rediff.com/news/2007/feb/10gaya.htm, last accessed on 6 November 2019

thirteen

The Nawada Jailbreak: A Tale of Two Gangsters

In 2007, a man named Ashok Mahto was arrested by the police on several charges including murder, and was regarded as one of Bihar's most dangerous criminal masterminds. Twenty months later, he was released. To their embarrassment, the police realized that they had caught the wrong man. So afraid were the police of this man, a hardened gangster, that they couldn't take the smallest of risks when it came to him. However, they seemed to have forgotten that the man they were looking for was already languishing in a prison in Bihar[1] and had been arrested a year before, in 2006. The only thing common between the two was their name. This case of mistaken identity was taken up by the state's Human Rights Commission, which ordered the state government to pay the man ₹2 lakh as compensation.

---

[1] 'Man Jailed Wrongly to Be Compensated', IANS, December 2009, http://www.sify.com/news/man-jailed-wrongly-to-be-compensated-news-national-jmbpubjhbcdsi.html

The real Ashok Mahto, a man responsible for over 40 murders, including that of an MP, ran one of the most dangerous gangs to have ever come out of Bihar. For nearly a decade, his rivalry with Akhilesh Singh, another gangster from the region, had come to define the violent politics of Nawada, a district in Central Bihar. Both had escaped from prison in 2001 that had left the district administration wild. So, when it came to Mahto and his arch nemesis, Singh, the police could never be too careful.

Mahto's story begins at the end of the twentieth century—in 1998—when he formed his own gang. But he really made a name for himself as one of Bihar's most notorious mafia lords in the early 2000s and that is where our story begins.

The first five years of the new century carried forward the violence that had come to grip Bihar in the 1990s. The state had become the arena of intense caste competitions and violence, a direct outcome of its long-established social order being challenged. The Bhumihars, the landowning, feudal caste that held control of the countryside up until the early '90s, found its authority challenged by the Yadavs, who, under the leadership of Lalu Prasad Yadav and his political party Rashtriya Janata Dal (RJD), had brought about a tectonic shift in the power equation of the state. This reconstitution of social hierarchy benefitted not only the Yadavs but also the other backward castes such as the Koeris, the Kurmis and the most backward of them, the Dalits. In some ways, it was simple arithmetic. The coming together of the bottom of the pyramid posed a serious challenge to the status quo and led to the unmaking of traditional authority. However, in 1994, a new political party came into being, which was led by Lalu's old friend and later his arch nemesis, Nitish Kumar, who stitched together a different social coalition that included the Koeris and the Kurmis along with the Bhumihars.

This caste coalition posed a challenge to Lalu's 'Muslim and Yadav' combination and worked on getting him out.[2]

In Nawada, the contestation between the Bhumihars and the Koeris took a violent form: a decade-long gang war between the two hoodlums—Akhilesh Singh was a Bhumihar and Ashok Mahto a Kurmi.

BHUMIHAR VS KURMI

It is said that over a hundred villages were affected by the rivalry between the two gangs. In 2003 alone, according to the district administration, 46 people had lost their lives because of the gang violence.[3]

While their conflict had been on since 1998, the tension between the two gangs really blew up in June 2000, where, in a matter of 15 days, the situation escalated to a point where bodies were dropping on both sides by the day. On 2 June, when Mahto's gang killed a Bhumihar man over a sand-mining contract, this was the beginning of the unending cycle of violence.

The next day, Akhilesh Singh's gang killed six Yadavs. Up until then, the violence in the district was limited to the Yadavs and the Bhumihars. Perhaps that is why Singh did not see Mahto's hand behind the murder involving the sand-mining contract and make an immediate call to arms. Even the local

---

[2] Salil Kumar, 'Lalu, Aloo and Baloo', Rediff.com, 3 February 2005, https://www.rediff.com/election/2005/feb/03spec.htm, last accessed on 31 January 2020

[3] Dipak Mishra, 'Singh-Mahto Crossfire Has Affected 100 Bihar Villages', *The Times of India*, 20 February 2003, http://timesofindia.indiatimes.com/articleshow/38007968.cms?utm_source=contentofinterest&utm_medium=text&utm_campaign=cppst, last accessed on 31 January 2020

press saw the two incidents as unconnected. The killing of the six young men was allegedly to send a clear message to those who had not voted for Singh's wife Aruna Devi, who was the sitting Member of the Legislative Assembly (MLA).

Nawada was then known as the land of 'Lalu, aloo and baloo'—the first reference to Lalu Prasad Yadav, the regional strong man, the second to the bountiful potato cultivation, and lastly, to the rampant illegal sand mining. But ever since the verdict was thrown up during the state elections of 2000, in which Aruna Devi was elected as an MLA, caste tensions began to grow. The killing of the six young men, by her husband, only made matters worse, and then the subsequent kidnapping and murder of three Kurmis was the tipping point. The events that took place in Afsar, a small village, on the night of 12 June 2000, would permanently change the landscape of Nawada.

On the midnight of 12–13 June 2000, nearly 50 men in paramilitary uniform entered Afsar and made their way to a house where 15 Bhumihars were sleeping on the terrace. Once they had surrounded it, their leader gave them the signal to start firing. As the victims lay writhing in pain, the gang, led by Ashok Mahto, slit their throats. Of the 15, 11 died instantaneously, including two young children of four and 10. The death toll hit 12 when another victim died in the hospital. Mahto was avenging the abduction and death of three Kurmis by Akhilesh Singh. One of the 12 killed was Singh's real brother Rajo Singh.[4] This was an act of war.

---

[4] Tapas Chakraborty, '12 Shot Dead in Bihar Midnight Massacre', *The Telegraph*, 13 June 2000, https://www.telegraphindia.com/india/12-shot-dead-in-bihar-midnight-massacre/cid/895371, last accessed on 6 November 2019

Mahto was now a wanted man, and the focus of the entire state's mechanism was on finding a way to arrest him, which finally happened later that year.

THE ESCAPE

On the morning of 23 December 2001, a Sunday, Nawada District Jail was overcrowded and understaffed. On this particular morning, there were four unarmed guards, four jail sentries and 1,100 prisoners.

A Tata 407, with four men inside, drove up to the prison gate. They told the guards that they had come to meet two of the convicts, Acchat Singh and Ashok Mahto. The request was sent to Amrendar Singh, the senior warden of the prison, who allowed them to be let in. During the trial of Pintoo Mahto, one of the aides of Ashok Mahto and fellow inmate, the Public Witness said that these visitors were carrying fruits and sweets.

Once the men crossed the jail's threshold, the plan to escape, which was hatched in utmost secrecy for over two months, was set in motion. The exit route was carefully thought through after taking into consideration the strength of the jail. They had gone through the sequence a hundred times so that the breakout was as seamless as possible. The prison guards had no idea as to what was coming their way. So when the Tata 407 came up to the gate and sought permission, no one noticed anything unusual.

The prison guards knew that the visitors were going to meet the butcher of Afsar and yet how easily they got permission reveals a startling fact about how prisons are run in India. Jails have a system of their own with their own currency and social status. The hierarchies in prison are based on the amount of money a prisoner can throw around. Money can ensure pornography magazines, home-cooked food and other perks such as regular meetings with friends and relatives.

Earlier that morning, Pintoo Mahto received his lunch-tiffin as he always did from his wife. She had packed him ladoos, some fish curry and a .38 revolver. The tiffin raised no suspicion, as it had passed through the hands of guards a hundred times in the past. As the smell of hilsa (fish) wafted through the cells, the guards gathered around the tiffin box and the sweets were generously distributed to them. They quickly gobbled up the ladoos without realizing that they were laced with rat poison.

The jail was staffed with unarmed wardens, jamadars (a minor official or junior officer) and a bada jamadar along with just four armed guards. After they consumed the poisoned sweets, they puked blood and were left immobilized.

Prisons are an excellent place to find new recruits, and Ashok had managed to do just that. He had expanded his gang and made new friends. Soon, Pintoo was to become one of Ashok Mahto's most trusted lieutenants. With the laddoos dispensed with, the first stage of the plan was complete/successful and now they waited to be busted out of the prison.

Meanwhile, the four men who had arrived in the Tata 407 were given permission to enter the prison and they made their way to the two prisoners.[5] Once inside the iron gates, the group pulled out their AK-47s and began firing blindly at the guards. It was no

---

[5] Amit Lodha, *Bihar Diaries: The True Story of How Bihar's Most Dangerous Criminal Was Caught*, Penguin (2018)

real contest; the guards with their government-issued .303 were slow in comparison to the automatic weapons carried by Ashok Mahto's accomplices. The deafening sound of the automatic gun rang through the entire jail. The sentries and others were caught with their pants down and retaliated clumsily. Shashi Bhushan Sharma, a sentry guarding the gate, began firing back. Out of nowhere bullets struck him and he crumpled to the ground. Lalan Prasad, the warden, too, picked up a gun and began firing at the men, but a bullet caught him in the arm and he collapsed. The assailants then picked up his gun and magazine and moved forward. Dhanusdhari Prasad Yadav, another jail guard, ran out to face the onslaught but due to the barrage of bullets, could not get past a certain point and ducked for cover.

'There was pandemonium in the prison,' according to the gate warden, Amarendra Kumar.[6]

Seven of the prisoners followed Mahto to where the getaway car had been waiting for them. Seizing the opportunity, Pintoo brandished his gun too. In the ensuing chaos, the prisoners began yelling at each other to hurry before the district police came. Right before he left the prison, Ashok Mahto went into the bathroom, took a gun and found the deputy warden hiding in the toilet. He looked him in the eye and riddled his body with bullets.

One of the assailants was shot and profusely bleeding, but he managed to get into the car, and the driver drove them into the distance.

Binod Kumar, who was posted in the town police station in Nawada, was not expecting much to happen on a Sunday.

---

[6]Pintoo Mahto vs State of Bihar, https://www.casemine.com/judgement/in/5811a537e691cb26fc4da930

Nawada was not considered a quiet posting, but it had mellowed down since Mahto had been imprisoned. When the wardens ran in and exclaimed that there had been an escape, he ran to the jail. He entered the prison and followed the trail of blood that led him to the body of the dead sentry. He passed the prison's gate, which was 20-feet long and 14-feet wide, through a small side gate. Kumar found blood tracks leading out of the jail and fruits and sweets were strewn all over its floor.

Immediately after the escape, the case was passed on to SP Dayal Pratap, who promptly followed up by launching a massive manhunt. The borders of the district were sealed to prevent any of the escapees from slipping through the police's dragnet. Almost immediately, the police succeeded when three of the escaped convicts were killed in an intense encounter not too far away from the jail, in the Kauakol police area.

A DIARY AND THE ESCAPE ROUTE

On 25 December, two days after the jailbreak, a diary was found in the jail, which contained the blueprint of the escape and plans of fleeing to Bangladesh. The Tata 407 was to be used to get them as far as Bokaro, which was 200 kilometres away from the jail. From there, with the help of other criminal networks operating in Bihar, West Bengal and Bangladesh, they would head to Sealdah and finally to Bangaon, a town 15 minutes away from the border. At Bangaon, they would use a rickshaw and make it across the border.

According to a report in *The Telegraph*, the entire sequence charted out in the diary was published. Right after the escape, the car that took them to Bokaro crashed into a tree, which really put a spanner in their plans, forcing them to steal a jeep and head into the Kauakol hills. Here, the police surrounded them, and an encountered ensued, leading to the death of three of the seven convicts.

Meanwhile, another angle that the diary threw up was a possible political nexus in facilitating the escape. The name and phone number of Raj Ballabh Prasad Yadav, the then state government's minister of labour, was found in the diary. The minister vehemently denied any role in the escape. When the press questioned Yadav, he showed indignation and said that he could not have been involved in such a case and incidentally was out of town (in Calcutta to attend a wedding) when it happened.[7]

Ashok Mahto managed to get out of the Kauakol encounter and continued to evade capture.

THE BLOODSHED RESUMES

After Mahto escaped from Nawada District Prison, the violence between the two gangs began to escalate. Singh and Mahto were going after each other with a renewed bloodlust, killing gang members and targeting each other's families. The worst affected were those who were the bystanders, who often got caught in the crossfire.

Between 1998 and 2006, nearly 200 people lost their lives because of the gang violence.[8]

---

[7] Muntazir Imam, 'Jailbreak Diary Exposes Cross-Border Nexus', *The Telegraph*, 25 December 2001, https://www.telegraphindia.com/india/jailbreak-diary-exposes-cross-border-nexus/cid/909176, last accessed on 6 November 2019

[8] HT Correspondent, 'Nitish's Record Gets Beating', *Hindustan Times*, 23 May 2006, https://www.hindustantimes.com/india/nitish-s-record-gets-beating/story-AdqNMkOeMQZib970lxtiiI.html, last accessed on 6 November 2019

One such incident of retaliation and senseless violence happened between 12 and 13 February 2003. On 12 February, five of Mahto's men were digging a hole in the riverbed in Dariyapur Ghat, when Singh's men caught and killed them. The next day, Mahto took swift revenge.

As the jeep slowed down at a turning in Kochgaon, Warisaliganj, the members of the Kurmi gang swooped down and blocked its path. They asked the women to step out of the vehicle and opened fire. Seven people were killed, including the local MLA Aruna Devi's father, Kailash Singh, several relatives of a minister of the mines in Jharkhand and another local MLA. All those who were killed were Bhumihars.[9]

CLEANING UP

Pradeep Mahto, the nephew of Ashok Mahto, was arrested for his role as one of the chief architects of the escape and was in and out of prison for the next 12 years. However, during this period, he defeated Akhilesh Singh's wife, Aruna Devi, in the elections in 2005 and 2010. In 2013, a local court sentenced him to life imprisonment for his alleged role in facilitating the escape, but he challenged it successfully.[10]

Pintoo Mahto was arrested in 2006 from Deogarh. After

---

[9] Special Correspondent, 'Jharkhand Minister Kin Killed in Bihar', *The Telegraph*, 16 February 2003, https://www.telegraphindia.com/india/jharkhand-minister-kin-killed-in-bihar/cid/838506, last accessed on 6 November 2019

[10] Press Trust of India, 'Man Sentenced to Life in 12-Year-Old Jailbreak Case', News18, 13 June 2013, https://www.news18.com/news/india/man-sentenced-to-life-in-12-year-old-jail-break-case-615765.html, last accessed on 6 November 2019

receiving a tip-off, the police found him living with his family in the region. They swiftly went in and arrested the man.

A month later, in 2006, the Bihar police, in an operation led by Amit Lodha, arrested Ashok Mahto again.

Akhilesh Singh, too, escaped from prison. He was arrested in 2000, when, much to the surprise of the patrolling police officers, they found the notorious gangster having pani puri on the side of the road. He was immediately nabbed and sent to prison. Though not long after, he managed to escape from prison after procuring forged bail documents. Another time, he managed to ditch his escort on the way to the court. Finally, destiny caught up with him in 2017, but it was not very clear as to how long he would be kept behind bars.

Even today, the shadow of the two gangsters looms large over the criminal network, and through it, the politics of Nawada. Both Singh's and Mahto's family members have won elections from the Warisaliganj seat. Once in a while, violence still flares up, proving that in India, it doesn't matter if one is in prison or elsewhere if one wants to carry out dangerous caste wars.

fourteen

Walking Out of Prison

There were 371 young political prisoners in Tihar's camp jail in May 1983. The daily roll call conducted by the warders had become a joke to the prisoners and the officers alike. In that queue also stood the 2019 Nobel Laureate Abhijit Banerjee![1] They would snigger as the names were called out. The prisoners would respond to obviously made-up names such as 'Gabbar Singh' or 'Khunkhar Singh' with a 'present' or 'yes' but never an 'absent'. A couple of days later, it became apparent that many out of the 300-odd detainees in the boys' barracks were missing; the sniggering turned into dread. The gaps in the lines were lapses in the security of Tihar Jail, the largest prison in South Asia. In over two days, 67 of the political prisoners detained from New Delhi's Jawaharlal Nehru University (JNU) escaped! The jail authorities were shocked. What was odd was that the number of attendees in the roll calls

---

[1] India Today Web Desk, 'When Nobel Laureate Abhijit Banerjee Spent 10 Days in Tihar Jail', *India Today*, 14 October 2019, https://www.indiatoday.in/india/story/nobel-laureate-abhijit-banerjee-tihar-jail-jnu-protest-1609360-2019-10-14, last accessed on 6 November 2019

never changed, but the number of students had visibly thinned out. So the question remained: how did these students escape India's largest maximum-security prison without being detected?

STATUTE 28 AND UNREST

These days, it is not odd to hear of students from prestigious universities creating a 'ruckus' and the government cracking the whip on them. Between the late twentieth century and early twenty-first century, there have been similar incidents of government crackdowns on dissenting students whose views differ from its own, and a growing wave of resistance by students against a clampdown on free speech and the breakdown of liberal order.

In the 1980s, the then PM, Indira Gandhi, thought that 'JNU had become a headache for her'.[2] In 2016, when the students of JNU protested against the government's clampdown after student leaders were falsely accused of chanting anti-national slogans,[3] they were labelled 'anti-national' and 'anti-India'. The sequence of events and circumstances were starkly different. The two protests that were decades apart weren't wholly different. What happened in 2016 was very similar to the contestation in 1983. The students in both instances fought against what they perceived to be injustice, and in both cases the government clamped down hard. As a civil liberties' leader, Amiya Rao had

---

[2] Chaman Lal, 'Cracked Mirror', *Economic and Political Weekly of India*, 18, no. 28, 9 July 1983

[3] India Today Web Desk, 'Forensic Experts Say Kanhaiya Video Was Doctored', *India Today*, 20 February 2016, https://www.indiatoday.in/india/delhi/story/forensic-experts-say-kanhaiya-video-was-doctored-309626-2016-02-19, last accessed on 6 November 2019

identified the problem JNU was going through in 1983 in her article in the *Economic and Political Weekly*. 'All the four pillars a university stands on—the Academician, the Administrator, the Student and the Karmachari—have developed cracks. Instead of attending to these, the continuous effort has been to cover them up. The clumsy patchwork has made the cracks only deeper and uglier.'[4]

The anger seething through the campus was as much Indira Gandhi's coterie's doing as it was the effect of the larger problems in the Indian education system. Years of nepotism, a lack of institutional accountability and rampant corruption had stymied the progress of JNU and taken it further away from the 'liberal' university that it had intended to be. Statute 28 of JNU had left enough ambiguity in the hiring processes and had been misused to provide employment to family members and close associates with considerable political and economic influence. These vagrancies on the part of the university's administration had been brought up in the Parliament. JNU's hostels were used for preparation of competitive exams, and the funds for research remained underutilized.[5]

Unrest was brewing due to a combination of forces, especially the relationship amongst students, teachers and the administration, and its causes were a chapter unto themselves. A newer type of student was entering the university, breaking the stranglehold that the elite had on 'admissions'. This newer class was viewed with suspicion. It was this departure from

---

[4]Amiya Rao, 'Image and Reality', *Economic and Political Weekly*, 18, no. 28 (9 July 1983): 1221–22 https://www.epw.in/journal/1983/29/our-correspondent-columns/jawaharlal-nehru-university-image-and-reality.html, last accessed on 6 November 2019
[5]Ibid.

the urban, elite class that had come to occupy the institute in its early years and this new wave of admissions found itself routinely judged by a section of the faculty and students as being incompatible to the ethos of the university. As these students were more vocal and assertive, they constantly raised questions on elitism and access, which accentuated the difference between the underperforming, elitist faculty and the student body.

DISSENT THEN AND NOW

On 27 April 1983, Jalees Ahmed, a student who was transferred from one hostel to another without proper justification, became the trigger for the brewing confrontation between the faculty and administration on one side and the student body on the other. The room was later locked. Disregarding the rules of the university, the president of the students' union, along with Ahmed and another office-bearer, broke the lock of the room and forced their entry. The teachers protested the flagrant violation of rules and threatened to boycott the exams. The vice chancellor of the university, P.N. Srivastava, expelled the two students, but this decision faced severe backlash from the students' body, which came together as a unit, charging the authority like a battalion of Roman soldiers.[6]

After both sides dug their heels in for a long battle, hundreds of students decided to gherao, or surround, the vice chancellor's house and held Srivastava and two other officials captive for over 50 hours. Attempts to defuse the situation failed, but the gherao came to a sudden end when the police entered the university at

---

[6]Jugnu Samasamy, 'Hostel Transfer of Student Leads to Violence in Jawaharlal Nehru University', *India Today*, 15 June 1983

the behest of the teachers' wives and the Lieutenant Governor of Delhi, Jagmohan.[7]

It was after 11 May that violence tore through the university. Police officers charged into the university to break up the *gherao*. They were able to free the three captives and went on a rampage in the university. They beat up several students and arrested 37 of them. One of the 37 arrested was Mukul Manglik, who is now a professor of history at Ramjas. Manglik, in a conversation with the author, recalls:

> I was in my hostel room in Kaveri when the news came that there was police action under way and students were being brutally beaten. When we heard the news, many of us left the hostel and marched to the site of the gherao. We wanted to protest at the police action. I happened to be at the head of the marchers, shouting slogans and demanding that the police leave the campus. Upon reaching the site of police action, I realized, all of a sudden, that the crowd behind me had all but dissolved. I was almost alone in the middle of a group of policemen, being savagely beaten and thrown around like a football in this circle. I clearly remember that I had my arms over my head to protect my skull while my body was being severely pummelled.

By the time Manglik got into the police van, a constable at the door pulled out a truncheon and hit him so hard that his shoulder blades went numb.

After the arrests, the entire students' body went berserk

---

[7]'Current Topics: The Great Escape: Students Fool Police', *The Times of India* (1861–current), 19 May 1983; ProQuest Historical Newspapers: *The Times of India*, pg. 8

and stoned teachers' houses, ransacked them and burnt books. However, the violence ended when the students themselves curtailed others. By 7 p.m., the violence abated but for sporadic instances that continued to erupt till 9 p.m.[8] According to news reports, the police returned later and a large number of students—many of whom were not even present on campus earlier—assembled on the lawns of Jhelum, one of the several hostels in JNU.

Nearly 500 students courted arrest, and were taken to Tihar. All of them went willingly, defying authority, protesting, singing songs of freedom and breathing togetherness. They thought that courting arrest would put pressure on the police and the administration, which would result in the release of the 37 arrested earlier. Although only 371 of the 500 were imprisoned, none knew what would happen next. They did not know how long their sentence would be, but assumed it would not last for more than a few days. First, they were kept as Category-C prisoners, or violent offenders, but were soon given the tag of political detainees. In the following days, 17 charges were slapped on the students, ranging from attempted murder to dacoity and arson.

Many of these students who were lodged in Tihar thought it was a transformative experience. Several have chosen to document the impact of those 10 days in newspapers all over the world,[9] including nobel laureate Abhijit Banerjee.

---

[8] Jugnu Samasamy, 'Hostel Transfer of Student Leads to Violence in Jawaharlal Nehru University', *India Today*, 15 June 1983

[9] Amitabh Mattoo, 'I Found My Place in Tihar Jail', *The Hindu*, 12 May 2013

TIME IN TIHAR

When the days continued without any sign of their release from jail, the students began mobilizing not only for their space and rights but also for other prisoners of all classes in the jail.

'We lived in two barracks, and in between was a muddy ground and behind us was another muddy patch,' said Amit Sengupta, who, six years later, in 1989, became the president of JNU—a position that elicits veneration from the current students and alumni long after they have graduated. 'We were all political prisoners, and would cook for ourselves and the B-class prisoners[10].' The students turned the jail into their own little world and tried to bring normalcy by organizing processions, singing songs, chanting slogans and even convening general body meetings!

The first struggle that the students faced from within the jail came about in the first two days itself. They fought to increase the amount of money spent on their food—as they were educated political prisoners, their level of literacy came with better dietary privileges—and their calorific allowance was increased by double. 'The food was awful in the first few days; the dal was watery and the rotis were rubbery,' said another former JNU student. This meant that the other inmates began to get better food too. This was three years before Charles Sobhraj escaped, so cooking was still allowed on Tihar's premises. Halwa,

---

[10] B-class prisoners are those who are non-habitual prisoners of good character. By social status and education, they belong to a superior mode of living and have not been convicted of premeditated violence, or serious offence against property.

dal, with the right consistency, and other items that they would share with other inmates were also made.

They also set up different committees such as the toilet-cleaning committee, the mess committee and the nukkad natak (street play) committee amongst others.

'We got a football to play,' said Sajal Mitra, the general secretary of the students' union. 'We would play amongst ourselves and with the other inmates.'

There was an initial demand that both men and women should be housed together, but the police would not have any of that. Letters would be regularly smuggled from the women's jail too.

Life had normalized to such an extent that they were reminded they were in jail only when they crossed a long corridor to go to the visitors' hall.

There were also instances of petty friendly thievery in Tihar. 'Chappals invariably would get lost,' complained Amit Sengupta. Mukul Mangalik narrated stories of how 'special' things would be brought by friends or family members from outside and these would become objects of desire. Sometimes things as common as a banana would be coveted or stolen.

When the students were processed for entry into Tihar, they did not want to surrender their original identification documents. The arresting officers also cognisant of the 'teaching-a-lesson' aspect of the arrests treated the students' incarceration similarly, with a softer touch and humour. Out of the 300-odd male students who were detained, several named themselves versions of Bipin Chandra and other faculty members they disliked in the university. Laughter could be heard every day at the roll call.

FRUSTRATION AND THE ESCAPE

Nearly 10 days passed and the students began to feel that there was no end to their imprisonment. Every day visitors from the university would throng to allay their fears; families and friends would come to the jail and spend time with those behind bars. Visitors would be stamped with ink, or a thappa (imprint), to show that they had arrived as guests.

The roll calls had become somewhat of a joke, as mentioned earlier. On the afternoon of 15 May, as usual the visitors came and left. When the counting was done in the women's jail, they found four girls missing. It turned out that the stamp that was put on the wrists of the guests could be easily transferred on to the wrists of the prisoners. Some reports also said that a few visitors carried fake stamps with themselves, which were used by the inmates and so the four women just waltzed out of prison! There was a hue and cry in the women's ward, and R.L. Khanna, the additional magistrate who was made in charge of the enquiry, promised strict action. Even in the jail that held the boys, some were missing.

'One of the committees that was set up in prison was the street play committee. We were just sitting around in prison and thought why not get that [street play committee] going,' remembers Mukul Mangalik. 'On the first day after the formation of this committee, three to four members of the "mandali" appeared to be missing and word began to spread that they might have run away. This information was kept under wraps, and when the roll call was taken, students proxied.'

That was when they realized that more than four people could escape at a time! Word spread that one should not delay, and before the guards could do anything about those missing,

63 students vanished from the jail the next day! The next time the roll was taken, everything became evident and the police and guards were left red-faced.

The escape was an outcome of police laxity, as described by the media, which happened during what was called 'the interviews', which the police poorly monitored.[11]

What came to be known widely as the 'great escape' could have been prevented. The deputy superintendent had chanced upon the discrepancies earlier, but did not raise an alarm, because he did not want to draw attention to the possibility of a jailbreak.

For those still in prison, the leniency that had been on offer suddenly vanished. The fun, the laughter and the moments shared with wardens and the bonhomie were no more. Those left behind were treated just like everyone else in prison and many who had been there still remember the transition clearly. The obvious fallout resulted from the student leadership that had emerged, who made it clear that if anyone even nursed thoughts of escaping, they would be hurt.

What is not so well known is the brunt faced by the wardens and guards. 'Those who are on duty when an escape happens go through hell,' Sunil Gupta, the former press relations officer at Tihar, told the author. 'They themselves become embroiled in the case, they are discredited and have cases slapped on them,' Gupta added.

Mukul Mangalik, Amit Sengupta and others did not escape but were released on bail later. Eventually, the cases were

---

[11]'Current Topics: The Great Escape: Students Fool Police', *The Times of India* (1861–current), 19 May 1983; ProQuest Historical Newspapers: *The Times of India*, pg 8

dropped, and things went back to normal. Looking back in time, Mangalik and others were critical of the way the students had protested, saying that there was no unanimity among the agitators on whether gheraoing the vice chancellor was the correct means to a legitimate end.

They eventually did come back. However, in the face-off between student power and administrative might, neither emerged the victor.

In the subsequent years, some of those jailed became civil servants, professors, journalists, academics, thinkers and now Nobel laureates. While one may not think that in spite of having escaped prison one might attain positions of power, the series of incidents that unfolded in 1983 proved otherwise.

fifteen

POW:
They Just Wanted to Go Home

There still stands outposts, fences and hollowed-out, unkempt, weed-infested camps in and around western UP where, in the aftermath of the Liberation War of Bangladesh in 1971, 93,000 Pakistani soldiers, who had surrendered to the joint forces of the Indian Army and Bangladesh's Mukti Bahini, were interned.

Mohammad Iqbal Mirza was one of those soldiers, who, for the next three years, along with his regiment, lived in an Indian prisoner of war (POW) camp in northern India.

In an interview with the Pakistan daily, *Dawn*, Mirza said that there were a fair number of successful escapes. The soldiers were unafraid. 'It was mostly younger officers who would attempt to escape. You tend to take more risks when you're young. We knew there were several people who were trying to dig a secret tunnel. They would cover the opening up whenever they weren't digging or when they felt it would be discovered.' The soldiers seemed oblivious to the fact that they could be shot or have their nails pulled out, he added.[1]

WAR AND THE PARTITION

The brutality of the Partition had carved undivided India into two nations and three regions. Pakistan was faced with the Sisyphean task of governing two territories, with two distinct ethnic and linguistic groups, which were thousands of kilometres apart. Until 1956, the newly formed country was still under the dominion of the British rule and problems started immediately after.

The integration of Pakistan as one nation faced serious challenges. The economic, political and social disparity between East and West Pakistan caused much unrest. The East, with Dacca as its capital, as it was then known, was the breadwinner. Its jute exports, lush agricultural land and riverine system received a measly return. 'The East Pakistanis have, over the years, earned the bulk of the country's foreign exchange with their jute exports, yet the majority of schools, roads, new factories and modern government buildings went up in the west.'[2]

In 1969, unable to control the internal unrest, General Ayub Khan resigned from the post of president and that led to the release of Sheikh Mujibur Rahman and other political prisoners, who were imprisoned in the Agartala Conspiracy Case. Charged with sedition, Rahman had become a national figure for the

---

[1] InpaperMagazine, 'Flashback: From Behind the Barbed Wire', *The Dawn*, 16 December 2012, https://www.dawn.com/news/771713, last accessed on 6 November 2019

[2] Robert S. Anderson, 'Impressions of Bangladesh: The Rule of Arms and Politics of Exhortation', *Pacific Affairs*, 49, no. 3 (Autumn 1976) pp 443–75

fight for autonomy and independence. Ayub Khan's successor, Yahya Khan, slated elections for late 1970, before which a natural disaster unlike any hit East Pakistan—half a million lives were lost to the Bhola cyclone followed by a tidal wave.[3]

The elections gave Rahman's political party, the Awami League, a thumping victory, and Zulfikar Ali Bhutto's Pakistan Peoples Party (PPP) came second. The lack of West Pakistan's effort to address the damage in East Pakistan in the aftermath of the natural disaster and the growing guerrilla network of Rahman's followers made it difficult to maintain control over the East. The situation was aggravated by the hijacking of an Indian commercial airplane by either four Bangladeshis or two Kashmiris, depending on the narrative you follow.[4]

The only way West Pakistan could rein its Eastern half was through brutal military repression. With a population that accounted for 55 per cent of Pakistan's total population, East Pakistan's demography was predominantly Bengali Muslims, after whom the second-largest religion was Bengali Hindus followed by other religions. They were patrolled by 80,000 West Pakistani soldiers, who were mainly Punjabis and Pathans.[5] The repression came in the form of rapes, pogroms and senseless violence that was mainly directed at the Hindu population, of which nine lakh had sought refuge in India.

---

[3] William J. Barnds, 'Pakistan's Disintegration', *The World Today*, 27 (August 1971): pp. 319–29

[4] 'Chronology of the Crisis Source', *Pakistan Forum* 1, no. 4 (Apr–May 1971), pg. 3, 8 October 2011, Middle East Research and Information Project, Inc. (MERIP) Stable. https://www.jstor.org/stable/2569064, last accessed on 6 November 2019

[5] Robert S. Anderson, 'Impressions of Bangladesh: The Rule of Arms and Politics of Exhortation', *Pacific Affairs*, 49, no. 3 (Autumn 1976) pp 443–75

The year of 1971 was fraught with violence and unrest. After a little over two decades, the fragile relationship between East and West Pakistan finally broke. For over nine months, East Pakistan was engulfed by civil war, and it resembled a tinderbox, threatening to hurtle the entire region into a full-fledged conflict. It did not take time for tensions to blow up, which led to India and Pakistan fighting their third full-scale war. Out of that violence, a new nation, Bangladesh, was born.

LIBERATION POWS AND A SLEW OF ESCAPES

After the two-week war, more than 70,000 soldiers and 20,000 civilians surrendered to the joint command of India and Bangladesh. This was another hurdle for the repatriation because Pakistan had not recognized Bangladesh as an independent nation and would not, till 1973.[6] The troops had surrendered in phases, and by early 1972, camps were set up by the Indian Army. Initially, there was an amicable relationship between the soldiers of the two countries until the hope of an early repatriation vanished almost immediately.

In the aftermath of the war, Pakistani soldiers were imprisoned in Indian jails or makeshift camps. For the next two years, these soldiers would stay in India and be used as a bargaining chip. The demand? An assurance of peace and recognition of Bangladesh as an independent country and an accord on Kashmir. The then PM Indira Gandhi leveraged the presence of the 93,000 POWs for a resolution and the demarcation of the Line of Control (LoC) in Kashmir. However,

---

[6]Ajit Bhattacharjee, 'Pakistan POWs in India: How Much Longer Must They Be Held', *The Times of India*, 19 January 1973

Pakistan did not give up its claim over the state of Jammu and Kashmir. Zulfikar Ali Bhutto's government used every diplomatic method to free the soldiers and even took the matter to the UN, claiming that India was violating the Geneva Convention.[7]

Indian news reports showed that there was growing public anger in India against the move to hold these soldiers for such a long time, as so much money was being spent to protect, clothe and shelter them.

Almost immediately, stories of the prisoners escaping captivity began emerging. The desperation amongst the Pakistani soldiers had reached a fever pitch. Despite being caught and told to stop, they would not listen—often being shot at or gunned down.

On 1 November 1972, two Pakistani senior officials were shot dead when they tried to escape from a camp in UP. The two officers were being taken to the hospital for a regular dental and eye check-up when they made a run for it, but their attempt failed and one Lt M.I. Rizvi was shot dead.[8]

On 13 January 1973, four POWs charged the gate of a camp and managed to get away. The soldiers patrolling the camp called for reinforcements and fired at the prisoners, killing all of them.[9] In another incident, 13 Pakistani prisoners had dug a tunnel in the Allahabad POW camp but were all caught.

However, more peculiar things began to happen. Indian nationals began aiding the escape of Pakistani POWs. In a question-and-answer session in the Parliament, the then Defence Minister, Jagjivan Ram, revealed that on 6 January 1973, a POW

---

[7]Ibid.
[8]Times News Network, 'Fatal Bid by Pak POWs', 1 November 1972
[9]Times of India News Service, 'POW's Escape Bid Foiled', 26 March 1973

had escaped from a train between Bareilly and Shahjahanpur, UP, and four Indian nationals had been arrested for helping them. Meanwhile, in April 1973, another Indian national was detained under the Maintenance of Internal Security Act (MISA).[10]

RECOUNT

Colonel Sudarshan Rathee sat in his well-lit drawing room in one of the many grey high-rises in Dwarka, an affluent suburb of India's national capital. The room had been recently redone, and the faint smell of paint still lingered in the air. Colonel Rathee is a well-built man of average height and now touching 70 but still walks over eight kilometres on the golf course daily. His grey hair was immaculately combed, clothes crisply pressed, and he carried himself with a stiff formality that had the 'army' written all over it. He seemed pleasant, welcoming and chatty. He chatted casually till pressed to talk about his time watching over the POWs after the 1971 war with Pakistan.

His regiment had returned from Bangladesh, and before they were to be sent back to their home postings, they were stationed at the Agra Central Jail, a large compound that was bounded by a 12-foot-long wall. The camp in Agra was the largest and held the most notorious POWs. 'Those who showed better behaviour were shifted to other camps,' Coloned Rathee told me.

As the conversation meandered, he began outlining what things were like in the internment camps, 'The prisoners were held in various war camps across northern India. The main camps were Agra, Ranchi, Ramnagar–Rampur, Meerut and

---

[10] Rajya Sabha Records, 164.100.47.5, accessed in June 2019

Bareilly,' said Colonel Rathee. He said that there were other camps that held POWs but could not exactly remember where they were. 'I was with the Agra prison and I witnessed two escape attempts. Those who tried to escape defied authority, but they were all delinquents. There was a distinction amongst the soldiers and their housing. Some were kept in cells while others lived in the barracks.'

According to him, the difference in living standards was based on rank—while officers were kept at the barracks, the soldiers were housed in tents, cells and other specially created areas. 'The Indian Army was cognizant of the internal hierarchy of the soldiers and a sense of sensitivity and respect was built into managing the prisoners. We would let the officers handle their own men, as sometimes entire regiments were captured.'

The reports from that time show how these camps were policed. The barracks were tightly guarded. They had a two-pronged fencing—inner and outer parameter fencing—and in between was a gap of 2 metres where Alsatians would roam at night and sentries would patrol during the day. Although most of the jails have now vanished, there are some remnants. A supermarket called Sanjay Place now occupies the spot where the Central Jail once stood.

As mentioned earlier, he had witnessed two escapes. The first incident took place when he was ferrying 35 officer prisoners from Agra to Ranchi. Amongst those whom he was transferring were two Special Forces officers of the rank of a captain.

Colonel Rathee took a gulp of water, which punctuated his thoughts, and looked straight at me, but clearly, his eyes were reliving the series of events that had taken place in 1973. He was unsure of the month when he had transferred the prisoners. 'We transferred the prisoners in a third-class bogey.

They were guarded by 18 men and two Junior Commissioned Officers (JCOs). In 1973, the train would go from Agra to Patna and then from Patna head to Ranchi after a day-long pit stop. The day would have to be spent in Patna.'

When the train entered the Patna station, after an overnight journey, a headcount was conducted and to the alarm of the officers, one prisoner was found missing. Despite the number of times the soldiers counted the prisoners, they were always short of one. 'The escape was hard to fathom,' said Colonel Rathee, 'as the bogeys had iron bars on the windows and sentry in the corridor. We found out that he had hidden an impune file. In those days, when injections were given, they had to be mixed. One glass impune held distilled water and another injection powder. The doctors would have to cut the glass with a small iron file. This Special Forces officer had nicked one file and used it to cut the iron bar of the windows in one night. He jumped out of the running train.

'The escape was quite ingenious,' Rathee held up an imaginary file and started cutting imaginary bars. 'He had cut the bar, stuck it back with black tape and kept an angucha, a thin towel, over it.

'On the next night, onboard the train from Patna to Ranchi, I was quite apprehensive that the other Special Forces officers might try to escape. At that point, we had not been able to understand how he had managed to escape,' continued the Colonel. 'During the day, I took my guards and conducted a drill near the railway station to keep them prepared. I was convinced that the other Special Forces officer would escape and had told my sentries that they should keep vigil and keep a watch on the side of the train.

'Sure enough, on the second night, the other Special Forces

officer tried to escape, but the non-commissioned officer shot him with a sten gun, carbine and 36 bullets. He fired nine rounds, out of which five hit the prisoner. I will never forget the name of the prisoner who was killed. His name was Shujaat Latif.'

At this point, Colonel Rathee paused again, crossed his legs and rubbed his thin long fingers, trying to find the words to narrate the rest of the story, 'I was in the regular bogey in the train when I got a call on the wireless about the prisoner being shot. While the train was hurtled ahead, I immediately pulled the chain and it stopped. I went to the engine driver and told him that the train had to go back; we went back for five kilometres. We located the body and he was still alive; we brought him back into the cabin of the train. The other prisoners were very scared. In the morning when we reached the railway station, we found the same thing. We found that the same bar had been removed and he had tried to escape from the same window.

'Meanwhile, the first prisoner who had escaped had been caught. We got information that he had been found lying unconscious by a railway gang-man and he had been put in a civil prison for a few days. We went back and fetched him. When he was brought back we found that he had cut his tongue.

'The news of the shooting of the prisoner reached Pakistan, who were using the UN and the Red Cross to exert pressure on the Indian government to release the 93,000 POWs. It was the prisoners who had filed a petition. They claimed that the second prisoner who tried to escape was deliberately shot dead by the guards and the petition was presented to the Red Cross. I, with my guard commander and the men, stayed back in Ranchi for one-and-a-half months while the investigations were underway. The Red Cross team came and found nothing amiss. The guard commander was awarded a medal.'

FALSE CEILING

It had been 20 minutes and Colonel Rathee, a little stiff from talking, moved to his dining table.

'When I was at the Agra camp watching over it, we would have roll calls four times a day. They were held at 6 a.m., 11 a.m., 4 p.m. and 8 p.m. After the last roll call, the lights would go out.

'One morning, the officers in the barracks found one prisoner missing. We called all the sentries who were on duty at night. The entire camp was checked. And we were at a loss for six hours, as we could not find him.

'Eventually, sniffer dogs were put into service; they would go up to the latrines and, thereafter, would lose direction. Despite the handler's attempt to take one of the dogs to the fence, the dog refused to move.

'Meanwhile, one of the sentries found something peculiar in the same barracks where this prisoner was living. He saw a false ceiling made of a square cardboard, held by an angle iron. When the cardboard was removed, the prisoner was found hiding in the false ceiling!'

By 1974, the prisoners were sent back to Pakistan. India won the war, but the government was rapidly losing public support. There is very little archival material and research that has been done on the time that these soldiers spent in the POW camps. There is no film and only a few books. There is a deafening silence of stories by the Pakistani soldiers. That is why Mirza's interview in *Dawn* is precious and provides us insight, albeit of a limited kind, into their perspectives. The abiding message of the interview is that they just wanted to go home, even if it meant dying in the process.

sixteen

Psycho Killer: Thank God He Is Dead

On 1 September 2013, Bengaluru was in a state of absolute panic. One of India's most feared serial killers and rapists had escaped from Parappana Agrahara Central Jail. The police issued an advisory for people to remain indoors. Posters were plastered all over the city and the police were snipping at the heels of the escaped convict. Could the police have stopped the escape? Perhaps. Just like in his criminal career, where he would leave breadcrumbs for the police to follow, M. Jaishankar had been apparently claiming within the walls of Bengaluru's most secure jail that it was only a matter of time before he would get out.

BLOODLUST

M. Jaishankar was a serial killer whose lust for killing seemed insatiable. Known as 'Psycho Shankar', his penchant for killing women was so strong that he used to carry a little black bag with a machete everywhere.[1]

On 3 July 2009, Shankar committed, or rather tried to commit, his first crime when he attempted to rape and murder P. Shyamala, a woman of 45, from Perandahalli, near Hosur in Tamil Nadu. Hailing from Salem district, he was working as a truck driver at that time.[2]

'She was taken to a hideout and the accused tried to rape and murder her,' said Hudco police, who investigated the case. She began to scream, and some locals heard her and rescued her. Jaishankar had escaped by then.[3]

This early phase of Jaishankar's career, in many ways, echoes that of serial killers from David Fincher's seminal television show, *Mindhunter*. The show chronicles the formation of the US government's Federal Bureau of Investigation's (FBI) Behavioural Science Unit, who coined the term 'serial killer'. The show follows Agent Holden Ford, a young officer, who interviews killers who display repetitive patterns and traits, to discover similarities in the method, process and psychology of the killers. Psycho Shankar mirrors the findings from the show: like an archetype typical 'serial killer'. He would leave

---

[1] DNA Correspondent, 'Bangalore: Watch Out, There's a Psycho On the Loose', DNA, 3 September 2013, https://www.dnaindia.com/bangalore/report-bangalore-watch-out-there-s-a-psycho-on-the-loose-1883827, last accessed on 5 November 2019

[2] TNN, 'M. Shankar Alias Jaishankar Has No Control Over Criminal Instinct', *The Times of India*, 2 September 2013, http://timesofindia.indiatimes.com/articleshow/22217646.cms?utm_source=contentofinterest&utm_medium=text&utm_campaign=cppst, last accessed on 5 November 2019

[3] TNN, 'Serial Rapist Gets 10-year Prison Term', *The Times of India*, 30 April 2013, http://timesofindia.indiatimes.com/articleshow/19794807.cms?utm_source=contentofinterest&utm_medium=text&utm_campaign=cppst, last accessed on 4 November 2019

breadcrumbs for the police that allowed them to learn from every crime. His profession would allow him to drive around and eventually he found his method of committing a crime through practice.

Shankar would lure sex workers from the highways to dhabas, befriend them, take them to the fields in the middle of the night, rape them and then kill them. He had 11 cases of rape and murder against him by the time he was arrested for the first time.

It was truly wondrous how brazen his attacks became. His first attempt at rape was foiled when the victim began screaming and he was caught and beaten. His second attack not only put him under the scanner of the police but also made him a wanted man. He kidnapped M. Jayamani, a 39-year-old police constable from Perumanallur, where she was on duty during the visit of the then deputy chief minister, M.K. Stalin. He abducted the constable in August 2009, and then until the next month, he, along with his partner, raped and then killed her. Her body was found on 19 September 2009. In the interim, more bodies were found and Shankar was trying to quench his insatiable thirst for rape and murder.

With the body count increasing and the discovery of the body of Jayamani, the state police was spurred into action who then immediately sent out a statewide search to nab the heinous murderer. They picked up on his phone calls; he had a habit of staying in touch with his family. The police were able to triangulate his location and nab him.

When they finally arrested him on 19 October 2009, they had no idea who they had caught hold of. As the interrogation proceeded, they found the depth of his crimes. Lucidly, without any display of guilt, he told them about the dozens of rapes, hundreds of robberies and the murders that he had committed. The police team was taken aback by his admission. Eventually, he was charged for eight cases of rape, three cases of murder, four cases of attempt to murder and one case of causing grievous hurt.[4]

In 2014, he was acquitted for the brutal murder of 50-year-old K. Thangammal Ponnaya of Thillaipuram in Namakkal town on 10 September 2009 at her farm. The police failed to collect and present the evidence to the court. Jaishankar and his accomplice P. Mohan Selvan had reportedly hacked the 50-year-old woman with a sickle, severed one of her limbs and stolen a chain weighing around 8.5 sovereigns.[5]

ESCAPE ONE

Between 2009 and 2011, the serial killer spent time in Coimbatore's Central Jail. On 17 March 2011, he was escorted to a hearing in Salem by two police constables, M. Chinnasamy and Rajavelu. The next day, when they were heading back to the Central Jail, he flatly refused to travel in anything but a super-deluxe bus. The ignorant and perhaps trusting constables went to buy the tickets from a bus stand. By the time they returned, he had escaped. The next morning, when the bus

---

[4] V.S. Palaniappan, 'Notorious Criminal Nabbed', *The Hindu*, 6 May 2011, https://www.thehindu.com/news/national/tamil-nadu/notorious-criminal-nabbed/article1994444.ece, last accessed on 4 November 2019

[5] Express News Service, 'Namakkal Court Acquits Jaishankar in Murder Case', *The New Indian Express*, 1 February 2014, http://www.newindianexpress.com/states/karnataka/2014/feb/01/Namakkal-Court-Acquits-Jaishankar-in-Murder-Case-570922.html, last accessed on 4 November 2019

reached Coimbatore, Chinnasamy, consumed by humiliation, reached the Police Recruit School grounds in the city and shot himself in the face, ending his life for fear of being reprimanded.[6]

Jaishankar made his way to northern Karnataka and later to Delhi. While in Karnataka, he first found himself in Chitradurga and Tumkur districts, and then made his way through the entirety of Karnataka. Over a period of 30 days, he satiated his crazy blood lust that had developed from being cut off from normal life. He raped and killed six women in Bellary, Karnataka, and murdered two persons in Dharmapuri, Tamil Nadu. The police had by then managed to trace him to Bengaluru, but he gave them the slip and made his way to Delhi, where he threw his cell phone away and disappeared into the chaos of the national capital.[7]

After Delhi, he headed towards Mumbai. By now it was the month of May, and the police begun to lose hope of ever arresting him.[8] He was taking them on a national tour. While Psycho Shankar carried his feral murderous streak with him, the officers carried guns and photos of the serial killer, which they pasted at public places with the hope of a tip-off that would help them apprehend him. They would get lucky only

---

[6] V.S. Palaniappan, 'Notorious Criminal Nabbed', *The Hindu*, 6 May 2011, https://www.thehindu.com/news/national/tamil-nadu/notorious-criminal-nabbed/article1994444.ece, last on accessed 4 November 2019

[7] TNN, 'Criminal Rapes, Kills 6 Women After Escape from Salem', *The Times of India*, 28 April 2011, https://timesofindia.indiatimes.com/city/chennai/Criminal-rapes-kills-6-women-after-escape-from-Salem/articleshow/8103461.cms, last accessed on 31 January 2020

[8] A. Subburaj, 'Coimbatore Serial Killer Traced to Mumbai', *The Times of India*, 3 May 2011, https://timesofindia.indiatimes.com/city/coimbatore/Coimbatore-serial-killer-traced-to-Mumbai/articleshow/8147595.cms, last accessed on 4 November 2019

a few days later when the serial killer would be arrested on 5 May 2011 for the second time.[9]

Jaishankar was on the run, jumping between state boundaries and evading capture. He had stolen a motorcycle near Chitradurga and another one on his way to his next safe spot, wherever that may have been, and stopped in a small village called Elagi.

Working in her field, Chandrakala Hotagi was by herself, and she caught the attention of the rapist. He stopped to ask her for water, but once he noticed that she was alone, he tried to rape her. In that moment, she called out for help to her husband, Prakash Hotagi, and his friend who were working nearby. They rushed to the spot when they heard her scream and caught the rapist! The villagers took him to the police, and on the way, beat Jaishankar to a pulp.

What is amazing is that the police were about to let him go with only a warning thinking the beating meted out by the villagers would have been enough. However, one of the officers on duty recognized him and contacted the authorities, who quickly verified him and put him behind bars.[10]

Whenever he was evading capture, Jaishankar toyed with the police. He would leave behind clues and bait them, always staying a step ahead—these are typical traits of a serial killer.

---

[9]DNA Correspondent, 'Bangalore: Watch Out, There's a Psycho on the Loose', 3 September 2013, https://www.dnaindia.com/bangalore/report-bangalore-watch-out-there-s-a-psycho-on-the-loose-1883827, DNA, last accessed on 4 November 2019

[10]Firoz Rozindar, 'This Family Fears Revenge by Serial Rapist', *The Hindu*, 2 June 2016, https://www.thehindu.com/todays-paper/tp-national/this-family-fears-revenge-by-serial-rapist/article5094958.ece, last accessed 3 November 2019

However, once behind bars, he was subject to treatment for psychiatric problems, and there was a lot of time for that. After all he was to spend 27 years in prison, at least 10 in one go. Recognizing the threat that he posed, he was interned at Parappana Agrahara Bengaluru Central Jail.

Like most of the jails in India, Parappana Agrahara Central Jail was overcrowded, messy and ridden with internal politics. While these problems were difficult to overcome, they were easy to manipulate. The Central Jail looks daunting as its grey granite walls stretch for over 40 acres, and in 2011, they were holding nearly 6,000 inmates. The prison only has a capacity of a couple of thousand, and it remains woefully understaffed.[11]

It was into this world that Jaishankar, a wily, hardened criminal, was thrown in, and he immediately began making plans to get out of there.

ESCAPE TWO

Psycho Shankar escaped from the Central Jail on 1 September 2013 and was rearrested on 6 September. A headline from 9 September 2013 that appeared in *The Times of India* said, 'Serial rapist-killer Jaishankar's escape tale still a mystery.'[12]

However, there were four things that seemingly worked for Jaishankar—his ingenuity, a man on the inside who helped him, the condition of the prison, and lastly, an act of God. All these helped him become the first person to ever escape from

---

[11]Debi Prasad Sarangi, 'Bangalore Jail: An Island of the Unwanted', *Deccan Herald*, 7 August 2010, https://www.deccanherald.com/content/86904/bangalore-jail-island-unwanted.html, last accessed on 4 November 2019

[12]*Murderpedia*, https://murderpedia.org/male.J/j/jaishankar.htm, last accessed on 5 November 2019

the jail since its inauguration in 1997.

K.V. Gagandeep, Inspector General of Police (prisons), spoke to the press in the aftermath of the escape, trying to make sense of what had happened and how. What he was certain about (something that comes up in every escape) was the role of an insider in the escape. He told the press, 'We learnt that Jaishankar escaped from the jail by climbing two 20-feet inner walls and the 30-feet outer wall between 2 a.m. and 4 a.m. I don't rule out insiders' role in his escape.'[13] Subsequently, 11 officers were suspended: three wardens, two jailors and six security guards who were on duty at the time of the breakout.

The other obvious factor that an inquiry cannot solve is the gross overcrowding of the prison, which held over 6,000 inmates with an original capacity of only 2,100. It took the staff of the jail over 12 hours to identify whether Jaishankar was actually missing or not. Another theory that went around was that it was not just because of the jail being understaffed, but also for deep fissures and camps present in the jail and its administration being run on caste and patronage. In many cases, prisoners were prioritized or looked after based on the caste of the administrator and that of the prisoner.[14]

It was a meticulously planned escape. On 31 August, Jaishankar was taken to Tumkur, some 80 kilometres from Bengaluru, for a hearing. On the way back, he began complaining about an uneasy feeling. Once back, he was admitted to the hospital within the jail. Things were falling into place for the

---

[13] Kestur Vasuki, '5 Days On, Runaway Serial Rapist Still at Large, Jail Staff Under Lens', *The Pioneer*, 6 September 2019, https://www.dailypioneer.com/2013/india/5-days-on-runaway-serial-rapist-still-at-large-jail-staff-under-lens.html, last accessed on 6 November 2019
[14] Ibid.

convict who had been planning this for over two months. 'He had a duplicate key to the hospital cell where he was locked up. He had noticed that guards came in every 30 minutes and knew he had 30 minutes to escape,' the then city police commissioner told the press.[15]

On that night, the rain lashed against the jail's grey walls. And at around 2 a.m., the lights went off and the jail plunged into darkness. Almost as if by the grace of the Almighty, Jaishankar made the first move to escape. He waited for the last guard to leave and then got out of his room using the duplicate key that he had.

According to prison officials, the Bangalore Central prison had 40 CCTV cameras, of which only eight were in working condition. This was when more than 50 high-value inmates needed constant monitoring.[16]

Once out of his cell, he made it down to the ground floor, where other high-profile prisoners were held, and found two gates open that led him straight outside. Now, it was just a matter of climbing three walls. The first was 30 feet high and the other two were 15 feet each. He came prepared to climb and received assistance from the oversight of the jail staff.

A large number of reports claim that the convict carried a bamboo pole with him, but he did not. He climbed up the

---

[15]TNN, 'Serial Rapist-Killer Jaishankar Planned Escape over Two Months', *The Times of India*, 8 September 2013, https://timesofindia.indiatimes.com/city/bengaluru/Serial-rapist-killer-Jaishankar-planned-escape-over-two-months/articleshow/22382895.cms, last accessed 6 November 2019

[16]PTI, 'Serial Rapist Killer Jaishankar Arrested Five Days after Sensational Escape,' India TV, 6 September 2013, https://www.indiatvnews.com/news/india/runaway-serial-rapist-arrested-near-bangalore-27499.html, last accessed 6 November 2019

walls with the support of a metal pole that held a jammer to prevent cell phone signal in the jail. Secondly, most jails have moats and rough terrains between the walls of the prison, but Parappana Agrahara had none of that. It was just an easy walk for him from one wall to the next. Over and above that, he was carrying medical rubber gloves to neutralize the electrified wires (which weren't actually needed because of the power cut) and bed sheets from his cell to climb over the wall.

However, the police said he injured his feet while crossing the connecting wall to reach the outer compound wall, as bloodstains were found on the walls and the ground below. Reaching the outer compound wall, the accused used a thick strap or belt from a duffel bag, tied it to the bottom of the electric fence and jumped 30 feet onto the ground. Running across an empty field, he must have reached the main road half a kilometre away, from where he disappeared.[17]

REARREST

Ten thousand posters and 75,000 pamphlets with different photographic profiles of Jaishankar were printed in Kannada, Tamil, Telugu, Malayalam, Marathi and Hindi and sent to Tamil Nadu, Andhra Pradesh, Kerala and Maharashtra.[18] Secondly, the

---

[17]'Prison Wall Not High Enough to Stop Serial Rapist', *Deccan Chronicle*, 2 September 2013, https://web.archive.org/web/20150714192448/http://archives.deccanchronicle.com/130902/news-current-affairs/article/prison-wall-not-high-enough-stop-serial-rapist, last accessed on 6 November 2019

[18]PTI, 'Serial Rapist Killer Jaishankar Arrested Five Days after Sensational Escape', India TV, 6 September 2013, https://www.indiatvnews.com/news/india/runaway-serial-rapist-arrested-near-bangalore-27499.html, last accessed on 6 November 2019

police began relying on its internal network of informants. The rapist had a large lead on them, but the police realized that he would not have got very far.

A police officer told a national daily that they 'were scouring every nook and corner of south-interior Karnataka and checking all categories of vehicles'. He said, 'We are in touch with police teams from Tamil Nadu and Andhra Pradesh. Our special teams have visited hotels, medical shops and eateries in bordering areas. But no one claims to have seen the fugitive.'[19]

The breakthrough came on the fifth day when Jaishankar called one of his associates and asked him for a car to escape in. The source immediately called the police, who were waiting for the escaped convict at the location in Kudlu Gate, a place five kilometres from the jail. It was true that he had hurt himself very badly; he had a limp and his feet were visibly swollen.[20]

He was rearrested and sent right back to the Central Jail.

Psycho Shankar spent the next few years on a wheelchair, slipping deep into depression. He took his own life in 2018.

---

[19] Kestur Vasuki, '5 Days On, Runaway Serial Rapist Still at Large, Jail Staff Under Lens', *The Pioneer*, 6 September 2019, https://www.dailypioneer.com/2013/india/5-days-on-runaway-serial-rapist-still-at-large-jail-staff-under-lens.html, last accessed on 6 November 2019

[20] T.S. Sudhir, Shreesha Reddy and Rohini Swamy, 'Psycho Shankar: How the Serial Rapist and Killer Was Nabbed,' *India Today*, 6 September 2013, https://www.indiatoday.in/india/south/story/psycho-shankar-how-serial-rapist-killer-was-nabbed-210165-2013-09-06, accessed on 6 November 2019

Acknowledgements

I would like to thank my family: Amma, Abba and Astha. I would also like to thank my colleagues and friends who, along the way, gave me advice, patiently listened to my stories and shared my excitement about all the characters I encountered. Lastly, the team at Rupa Publications, without whom this book would not have been possible.